Euthyde

PLATO

Euthydemus

Translated, with an Introduction, by
ROSAMOND KENT SPRAGUE

Hackett Publishing Company
Indianapolis/Cambridge

Plato: ca. 428–347 B.C.

Originally published in 1965 by The Bobbs-Merrill Company, Inc.

New material Copyright © 1993 by Hackett Publishing Company, Inc.

Printed in the United States of America

99 98 97 96 95 94   2 3 4 5 6 7

Cover design by Listenberger Design & Associates

For further information, please address

Hackett Publishing Company, Inc.
P.O. Box 44937
Indianapolis, Indiana 46244-0937

Library of Congress Cataloging-in-Publication Data

Plato.
    [Euthydemus. English]
    Euthydemus/Plato; translated, with an introduction, by
Rosamond Kent Sprague.
        p.   cm.
    Originally published: Indianapolis: Bobbs-Merrill, 1965. With
updated bibliography.
    Includes index.
    ISBN 0-87220-235-6 (alk. paper).   ISBN 0-87220-234-8 (pbk.:
alk. paper)
        1. Logic—Early works to 1800.   2. Methodology—Early works
to 1800.   I. Sprague, Rosamond Kent.   II. Title.
B369.A5S7   1993
160—dc20   93-14427
                                                       CIP

CONTENTS

Introduction

The *Euthydemus* is the dialogue of Plato's in which his gifts for comedy and satire are most apparent. It can be read with keen enjoyment as a brilliant attack on eristic sophistry, as well as studied with profit for the light it casts both upon ethical questions of the sort discussed in the early and middle dialogues and upon logical questions of the sort discussed in the later dialogues. The *Euthydemus* seems likely to belong to the period between Plato's first Sicilian visit in 388/7 B.C. and the writing of the *Republic*, perhaps about 380. In the same period probably fall the *Gorgias, Menexenus, Meno, Phaedo, Cratylus,* and *Symposium,* not necessarily in that order.[1] The dramatic date would be about 405; Socrates is elderly and Alcibiades (referred to as still alive at 275A) died in 404.

In form the *Euthydemus* is a reported dialogue with an outer frame (271A–275D and 304C–307C). Socrates describes to his old friend Crito an encounter he has had on the preceding day with two elderly sophists, Euthydemus and his brother Dionysodorus. He gives an account of five distinct scenes, in three of which (275D–278E, 283B–288D, and 293B–304B) the sophists take the lead, whereas in the two remaining scenes (278E–283B and 288D–293A) he is himself the chief speaker. (An interruption by Crito occurs at the end of the fourth scene, at 290E–293A).[2]

---

[1] This dating of the dialogue in general follows J. V. Luce, "The Date of the *Cratylus,*" *American Journal of Philology,* LXXXV, No. 2 (1964), 154. For a dating of about 390/89, see R. S. Bluck, *Plato's 'Meno'* (Cambridge, 1961), p. 115.

[2] The form and characters of the dialogue are particularly well treated by Paul Friedländer, *Plato: The Dialogues (First Period),* trans. Hans Meyerhoff (New York, 1964), pp. 179-95, and by Louis Méridier in his Introduction in the Budé edition (Paris, 1931), pp. 112-124.

vii

Plato's purpose in the *Euthydemus* is to champion the Socratic dialectic as against its false imitation, eristic, or con-
tentious reasoning. The structure of the dialogue is intimately
connected with this purpose, for each of the Socratic scenes is
sandwiched between two of the scenes in which the sophists are
shown displaying their eristic skill. When Socrates is in command, a young man, Cleinias, makes steady and even astonish-
ing progress toward the conclusion that the choice of wisdom is
a necessary means to happiness; the logical antics of the sophists,
however, are represented as being of no educational value whatsoever. By the way in which he has juxtaposed the two methods,
Plato has forced a comparison between them.

Plato must have been even more anxious to differentiate his
master Socrates from sophists of the eristic type than to dis-
tinguish him from more distinguished figures such as Protagoras
and Gorgias, for the brief question-and-answer method employed by Euthydemus and his brother has much more in common with the Socratic dialectic than with the lengthy style of
speech preferred by the other sophists.[3] There are echoes of
Socrates too when, in Scene V, our sophists talk of oxen, sheep,
the cook, the smith, and the potter.[4]

The origin of the eristic type of sophistry is obscure; some
have even supposed that it can only have arisen as a development of Socrates' own method.[5] In this case, Plato would be
depicting an atmosphere more nearly contemporary with himself than with Socrates and would perhaps be attributing to
Euthydemus and Dionysodorus some of the arguments of An-

---

3 Plato's Protagoras was exceptional, as indeed was Socrates, in being able
to use both styles (*Protagoras* 329B), but to Gorgias the lengthy style was
certainly more congenial (*Gorgias* 449C). The same appears to have been
true of Prodicus and Hippias.

4 This point was made by H. Sidgwick, "The Sophists," *Journal of Philology*, IV (1872), 298n.

5 *Ibid.*, IV (1872), 288 ff., and V (1874), 66 ff.; and also the comments
by E. S. Thompson in Excursus V of his edition of the *Meno* (London, 1901),
pp. 272–285. (The entire excursus is devoted to the subject of eristic, and
there are also some remarks on the subject in Thompson's note on *Meno*
80D, pp. 113–116.)

tisthenes or Euclid of Megara.[6] There seems, however, to be no doubt that the two sophists were historical persons, and we know of at least one sophism attributed to Euthydemus that is not in our dialogue;[7] this suggests that they were quite capable of committing their own fallacies. Thus, unless we are to assume that the Socratic dialectic became debased in Socrates' own lifetime (which is not at all impossible), we are entitled to look elsewhere for the origin of eristic. The most obvious alternative source is Parmenides, whose monism had already resulted in Zeno's paradoxes of motion. The yes-or-no form of question consistently employed by the sophists in the *Euthydemus* suggests the Eleatic mode of argument with its denial of a middle ground between being and not-being, for instance; and the fallacious arguments of Scene III include one, the argument against false speaking, which Plato associates with Parmenides in the *Sophist* (237A). Whatever the origin of eristic, it proved to be long-lived and was still of interest to Aristotle in his *On Sophistical Refutations*.

The *Euthydemus* has a special contribution to make to one very difficult question, that of Plato's consciousness of fallacy. When logical fallacies occur in the mouth of Socrates, as they often do in the dialogues, it may be difficult to decide if Plato understood them or not. The fallacies of the *Euthydemus*, however, are so obviously associated with sophists whom Plato regards with scorn, and so obviously cleared up by Socrates, that it is possible to study them in relative isolation from this difficulty. Thus, a close reading of the *Euthydemus* forms an excel-

---

6 The most sensible remarks on these two controversial persons are those of G. C. Field in *Plato and His Contemporaries* (London, 1930), pp. 160–174.

7 The Dionysodorus of Xenophon, *Memorabilia* III. 1. 1 is probably our Dionysodorus, and Euthydemus is mentioned by Aristotle in *On Sophistical Refutations* 177b12 ff. and *Rhetoric* 1401a26 ff., the same passages in which the sophism is described. (This sophism, involving a trireme and the Piraeus, is not quite the same in the two passages; on the resulting confusion, see Cope and Sandys' edition of the *Rhetoric*, II [Cambridge, 1897], 307–308. J. H. Freese's note on the second passage in the Loeb Classical Library edition is also helpful). Euthydemus is also mentioned again by Plato at *Cratylus* 386D.

lent introduction to the general topic of fallacy in Plato, a topic which has been far too often neglected in spite of its relevance to, say, the theory of Forms.[8] Summaries of the *Euthydemus* are numerous; to include one here seems unnecessary.[9] Instead we may consider some points of particular philosophical interest and suggest some questions arising from them:

1. *Can virtue be taught?* The sophists claim that they are able to teach it (273D) and also that the art by which they do so (eristic) is able to persuade a man that virtue can in fact be taught and that they are its best teachers (274E). But later (282C) we see that it is dialectic, not eristic, which produces in Cleinias the conviction that virtue (wisdom) is teachable. *Questions:* Has the *Euthydemus* some light to cast on discussions of the same topic in the *Protagoras* and *Meno?* Is there any significance in the fact that virtue and wisdom are used interchangeably in the *Euthydemus?* What is the import of Socrates' inquiry whether the art that teaches virtue can provide its own credentials (274E)? Is this a kind of reflexive situation which arises in other connections, say at *Gorgias* 459D ff.? (See below, p. 17, note 13). Has this reflexivity anything to do with the difficulties that always attend the search for a master art (291B ff.)? With those that accompany the sophist's argument against false speaking (287A)?

2. *Equivocation.* Following a series of sophistical refutations (275D–277C), Socrates gives a clear explanation (277E ff.) of their source: that "learn" has two senses enables it to be applied both to the man who knows and to the man who does not. *Questions:* Does this passage imply that Plato had a general understanding of equivocation and its connection with fallacy, or only of this particular equivocation? If the former, can anything be deduced about passages in other dialogues in which

---

8 For an extended discussion of this whole subject see R. K. Sprague, *Plato's Use of Fallacy: A Study of the Euthydemus and Some Other Dialogues* (London, 1962).

9 Summaries are contained, for instance, in the works cited in the Bibliography, p. xv, by Friedländer, Gifford, Méridier, Shorey, Sprague, and Taylor.

equivocations occur but are not explained? Does Plato have methods of exposure which are indirect? What are they? Is one of them employed by Socrates at 293C ff., where he adds qualifications to a number of the sophists' questions?

3. *Goods and the use of goods.* At 281DE Socrates says that the things which are normally called goods (279A ff.) are of no value in themselves; if they are guided by wisdom they are greater goods than their opposites, but if they are guided by ignorance they are greater evils. *Questions:* Has this passage some significance for the paradoxes in the *Hippias Minor* (that the good man is the man who errs voluntarily) and in *Republic* I (that the just man is the best thief)? And for the passages in the *Gorgias* comparing the misuse of rhetoric to the misuse of boxing (456C ff. and 460CD)? Is Socrates' argument in the *Euthydemus* an adequate proof that wisdom is the only good (281E)? And has he given any basis for his assumption that the good, if known, must be chosen (282AB)?

4. *The copula.* The argument at 283CE appears to depend on a shift from "is not wise" to "does not exist." *Question:* What significance has this passage for recent discussions of the copula in the *Sophist?* (See below, p. 22, note 31.)

5. *False speaking.* At 283E ff. the sophists argue against the possibility of false speaking on the ground that a lie must be about something that is, and whoever speaks what is speaks the truth. Furthermore, they say, it is impossible to speak what is not. *Questions:* How should the argument be analyzed? (See below, p. 24, note 35.) What exactly does Plato mean by saying (286C) that it upsets itself? How is the passage related to *Cratylus* 385B ff. and 429C ff.? To *Republic* V, 477A ff.? To *Theaetetus* 189A ff.? To *Sophist* 240D ff.?

6. *The search for the art which makes us happy.* One requirement laid down is that this art be a kind of knowledge that combines making and knowing how to use the thing made (289B). A number of arts fail to meet this requirement because the persons who make the things in question (for example, flutes) are not those who know how to use them. But the art that is the

most likely candidate, the kingly art, fails on a different ground; it does not appear to make anything at all (292A). Even if it confers the knowledge of itself, it is difficult to see of what use this knowledge can be. For instance, if the art is defined as "that by which we shall make others good" (292D), there is no obvious respect in which these others are made good; an infinite regress results, in fact. *Questions:* Is the failure of the kingly art to be the art which makes us happy a real or an apparent failure? Are the reasons for the failure to be found in Socrates' use of the *techne*-analogy, with its demand for a recognizable product? Is there some connection between the suggestion that this knowledge might confer knowledge of itself (292D) and the similar reflexive situation with regard to temperance in the *Charmides* 166B ff.? Is there some connection between the regress here and the regress concerning the friend at *Lysis* 219B ff.?

7. *Same, other, and not.* In a series of arguments beginning at 297E the sophists bring off their refutations by means of a systematic abuse of these terms. *Questions:* What significance has this passage for the discussion of the *megista genē* in the *Sophist?* Is 301AC also relevant in this connection?

8. *Parousia.* At 301A Dionysodorus has asked Socrates a question concerning the relationship between the beautiful and beautiful things. When Socrates answers that the beautiful things are different from the beautiful itself but that there is some beauty present with each of them, Dionysodorus proceeds to ridicule Socrates' answer by replying, "then if an ox is present with you, you are an ox?" *Questions:* Would Dionysodorus' objection be answered by the discussion of *parousia* in the *Lysis* 217B ff.? Is his remark in any way comparable to the objections to the theory of Forms raised in the first part of the *Parmenides?* If so, how would this affect certain interpretations of those objections?

9. *Self-predication.* At 301A Dionysodorus has questioned whether the different can be different. Socrates offers to solve this difficulty (which appears to have been raised as an objec-

tion to the theory of Forms) by saying, in effect, Why not? Isn't the beautiful beautiful and the ugly ugly? *Questions:* What weight is to be attached to Socrates' remark, "I was so eager to have the wisdom of the pair that I was already trying to copy it" (301B)? Is Plato making a distinction between legitimate Forms and some other sort? What significance has the whole passage 300E–301C for the current discussions of self-predication in Plato? (See below, p. 55, note 95.)

It should not be supposed that none of these questions has been studied;[10] they are raised here in order to give some indication of the philosophical richness of the dialogue and with a view toward stimulating interest in it. The current revival of studies in the history of logic, together with the present tendency of Platonic studies toward concentration on the problems prominent in the later dialogues (a number of which receive some treatment in the *Euthydemus* also) are indications that such interest is likely to increase.

In reading the *Euthydemus* it is essential to bear in mind that the fallacious arguments in the dialogue depend for the most part on peculiarities of Greek vocabulary, idiom, and syntax which are extremely difficult to reproduce in English. The Greekless reader is advised to keep a constant eye on the notes, where an attempt is made to explain these peculiarities as they occur.

The translation follows Burnet (Oxford Classical Texts) except as otherwise noted. Abbreviations in the textual notes follow the customary form: manuscripts are referred to by letters (B, T, or W) and previous editors by surnames (Badham, Heindorf) as in Burnet's *apparatus criticus*. Discussions of the few variants adopted will usually be found in the notes to the invaluable edition of E. H. Gifford (Oxford, 1905).

I wish to thank the American Council of Learned Societies

---

[10] The recent self-predication discussion, however, does seem to have bypassed the *Euthydemus* altogether. See below, p. 55, note 95.

for a Grant-in-Aid which enabled me to finish this piece of work. I am also indebted to two readers of the manuscript, Professor Glenn R. Morrow and Professor Robert G. Hoerber, for many valuable suggestions.

ROSAMOND KENT SPRAGUE

Calais, Vermont
June 1965

Selected Bibliography

BURNET, JOHN. *Platonis Opera.* Volume III. "Oxford Classical Texts." Oxford, 1903. Reprinted, 1957.

CANTO, MONIQUE. *L'Intrigue Philosophique: Essai sur l'Euthydème de Platon.* Paris, 1987.

CANTO, MONIQUE. *Platon: Euthydème.* Translation, introduction, and notes. Paris, 1989.

CHANCE, THOMAS H. *Plato's 'Euthydemus': Analysis of What Is and What Is Not Philosophy.* Berkeley, 1992.

FRIEDLÄNDER, PAUL. *Plato: The Dialogues (First Period).* Translated by HANS MEYERHOFF. New York, 1964. Pp. 179–195.

GIFFORD, EDWIN HAMILTON. *The Euthydemus of Plato.* With revised text, introduction, notes, and indexes. Oxford, 1905.

GUTHRIE, W.K.C. *A History of Greek Philosophy* IV. Cambridge, 1975. Pp. 266–283.

HAWTREY, R.S.W. *Commentary on Plato's Euthydemus.* Philadelphia, 1981.

HINRICHS, GERARD. "The *Euthydemus* as a Locus of the Socratic Elenchus," *New Scholasticism,* XXV, No. 2 (1951), 178–183.

KEULEN, HERMANN. *Untersuchungen zu Platons Euthydem.* Wiesbaden, 1971.

KNEALE, WILLIAM and MARTHA. *The Development of Logic.* Oxford, 1962. Chapter 1, section 4.

MÉRIDIER, LOUIS, ed. *Euthydème,* in "Collection des Universités de France." Budé Edition. Paris, 1931.

MOHR, RICHARD. "Forms in Plato's *Euthydemus,*" *Hermes,* 112 (1984), 296–300.

NARCY, MICHEL. *Le Philosophe et son Double: un Commentaire de l'Euthydème de Platon.* Paris, 1984.

SCOLNICOV, SAMUEL. "Plato's *Euthydemus:* A Study on the Relations between Logic and Education," *Scripta Classica Israelica,* 8 (1981), 19–29.

SHOREY, PAUL. *What Plato Said.* Chicago, 1933. Pp. 160–168.

SPRAGUE, ROSAMOND KENT. *Plato's Use of Fallacy: A Study of the Euthydemus and Some Other Dialogues.* London, 1962.

STRAUSS, LEO. "On the *Euthydemus,*" *Interpretation,* 1 (1970), 1–20.

TAYLOR, A. E. *Plato: The Man and His Work.* London, 1926. (6th edition reprinted 1949.) Pp. 89–102.

TELOH, HENRY. *Socratic Education in Plato's Early Dialogues.* Notre Dame, 1986. Chapter 12, "The Serious Man in the *Euthydemus.*"

WATERFIELD, ROBIN. *Euthydemus.* Translation, introduction, and notes, in *Early Socratic Dialogues,* ed. Trevor J. Saunders. Penguin Classics, 1987.

WELLS, GEORGE HENRY. *The Euthydemus of Plato.* With an introduction and notes. London, 1881.

EUTHYDEMUS

Euthydemus

Crito. Who was it, Socrates, you were talking to in the Lyceum yesterday? There was such a crowd standing around you that when I came up and wanted to listen, I couldn't hear anything distinctly. But by craning my neck I did get a look, and I thought it was some stranger you were talking to. Who was it?

Socrates. Which one are you asking about, Crito? There was not just one, but two.

Crito. The person I mean was sitting next but one to you on your right—between you was Axiochus' young son.[1] He seemed to me, Socrates, to have grown tremendously, and to be almost of a size[2] with our Critobulus. But Critobulus is thin, whereas this boy has come on splendidly and is extremely good-looking.

Socrates. Euthydemus is the man you mean, Crito, and the one sitting next to me on my left was his brother, Dionysodorus —he, too, takes part in the discussions.

Crito. I don't know either of them, Socrates. They are another new kind of sophist, I suppose. Where do they come from, and what is their particular wisdom?

Socrates. By birth, I think, they are from this side, from Chios. They went out as colonists to Thurii[3] but were exiled from there and have already spent a good many years in this region. As to your question about the wisdom of the pair, it is marvelous, Crito! The two are absolutely omniscient, so much so that I never knew before what pancratiasts really were. They

---

[1] The elder Alcibiades had two sons, Axiochus and Cleinias, whose sons were, respectively, our Cleinias and the famous Alcibiades. These last two were therefore first cousins, as is explained below at 275AB.

[2] Or possibly, "of an age."

[3] In 444/3 B.C., Pericles sent a colony to Thurii, on the Gulf of Tarentum. The laws for the new colony are said to have been written by Protagoras (Diogenes Laertius, IX. 50).

are both absolutely all-round fighters, not like the two battling brothers from Acarnania who could only fight with their bodies.[4] These two are first of all completely skilled in body, being highly adept at fighting in armor and able to teach this skill to anyone else who pays them a fee; and then they are the ones best able to fight the battle of the law courts and to teach other people both how to deliver and how to compose[5] the sort of speeches suitable for the courts. Previously these were their only skills, but now they have put the finishing touch to pancratistic art. They have now mastered the one form of fighting they had previously left untried; as a result, not a single man can stand up to them, they have become so skilled in fighting in arguments and in refuting whatever may be said, no matter whether it is true or false.[6] So that I, Crito, have a mind to hand myself over to these men, since they say that they can make any other person clever at the same things in a short time.

Crito. What's that, Socrates? Aren't you afraid that, at your age, you are already too old?

Socrates. Far from it, Crito—I have enough example and encouragement to keep me from being afraid. The two men themselves were pretty well advanced in years[7] when they made a start on this wisdom I want to get; I mean the eristic sort. Last year or the year before they were not yet wise. My only anxiety is that I may disgrace the two strangers just as I have already disgraced Connus the harpist, Metrobius' son,[8] who is

4 The pancration was a combination of wrestling and boxing. In this passage Plato exploits the literal meaning of the word, which is "all-round fighting." Nothing appears to be known of the two Acarnanian brothers.

5 A letter from Professor George Kennedy encourages me to differ with Liddell and Scott (*Greek-English Lexicon*, revised edition by H. Stuart Jones [Oxford, 1940]) in their interpretation of συγγράφεσθαι here.

6 The text reads "false or true," but here and in other similar cases the terms have been reversed to correspond to more usual English order.

7 There is a suggestion here that Euthydemus and Dionysodorus are "late-learners" like those described at *Sophist* 251BC. (That the pair are elderly may also be inferred from Ctesippus' remark about the number of their teeth at 294C.) Whether they are to be associated with the view of predication described in the *Sophist* is, however, still an open question.

8 Socrates also refers to Connus as his instructor in music at *Menexenus* 235E.

still trying to teach me to play. The boys who take lessons with me laugh at the sight and call Connus the "Old Man's Master." So I am afraid that someone may reproach the strangers on the same score; perhaps they may be unwilling to take me as a pupil for fear that this should happen. So, Crito, I have persuaded some other old men to go along with me as fellow pupils to the harp lessons, and I shall attempt to persuade some others for this project. Why don't you come along yourself? We will take 272D your sons as bait to catch them—I feel sure that their desire to get the boys will make them give us lessons too.

Crito. I have no objection, Socrates, if you really think well of the plan. But first explain to me what the wisdom of the two men is, to give me some idea of what we are going to learn.

Socrates. You shall hear at once, since I can't pretend that I paid no attention to the pair. As a matter of fact, I did just that and remember what was said and will try to recount the whole thing from the beginning. As good luck would have it, I was E sitting by myself in the undressing-room just where you saw me and was already thinking of leaving. But when I got up, my customary divine sign[9] put in an appearance. So I sat down again, and in a moment the two of them, Euthydemus and 273A Dionysodorus, came in, and some others with them, disciples of theirs, who seemed to me pretty numerous. When the pair came in, they walked round the cloister, and they had not yet made more than two or three turns when in came Cleinias, who, as you rightly say, has grown a lot. Following him were a good many others, lovers of his, and among them Ctesippus, a young man from Paeania[10]—he's a well-bred fellow except for a certain youthful brashness. From the doorway Cleinias caught B sight of me sitting alone and came straight up and sat down on my right, just as you describe it. When Dionysodorus and Euthydemus saw him, at first they stood talking to each other and glancing at us every so often (I was keeping a good eye on them) but after a while they came over and one of them, Euthydemus, sat down next to the boy, and his brother next

9 This is the *daimonion* of *Apology* 31D and *Phaedrus* 242B.
10 A deme of Attica.

to me on my left, and the rest found places where they could.[11]

273C Since I hadn't seen the two for quite a time, I gave them a good welcome, and then I said to Cleinias, You know, Cleinias, that the wisdom of these two men, Euthydemus and Dionysodorus, has to do with important matters and not mere trivia. They know all about war, that is, the things a man ought to know who means to be a good general, such as the formations of troops and their command and how to fight in armor; and besides this, they can make a man capable of looking out for himself in court if anyone should do him an injury.

D They obviously thought little of me for saying this, because they both laughed and glanced at each other, and Euthydemus said, We are not any longer in earnest about these things, Socrates—we treat them as diversions.

I was astonished and said, Your serious occupation must certainly be splendid if you have important things like these for your diversions! For heaven's sake, tell me what this splendid occupation is!

Virtue, Socrates, is what it is, he said, and we think we can teach it better than anyone else and more quickly.

E Good heavens, I said, what a claim you make! Wherever did you find this godsend? I was still thinking of you, as I just said, as men particularly skilled in fighting in armor, and so I spoke of you in this way. When you visited us before, I remember that this was what you claimed to be. But now if you really have this other wisdom, be propitious—you see, I am addressing you exactly as though you were gods because I want you to forgive
274A me for what I said earlier. But make sure, Euthydemus and Dionysodorus, that you are telling the truth—the magnitude of your claim certainly gives me some cause for disbelief.

Rest assured, Socrates, that things are as we say.

Then I count you much happier in your possession of this wisdom than the Great King in that of his empire! But tell me just this: do you plan to give a demonstration of this wisdom, or what do you mean to do?

11 Later, at 297CD, we are intended to remember where the two sophists are sitting.

We are here for that very purpose, Socrates: to give a demonstration, and to teach, if anyone wants to learn. 274B
I give you my word that everyone who does not have this wisdom will wish to have it: first myself, then Cleinias here, and, in addition to us, this fellow Ctesippus and these others, I said, pointing to the lovers of Cleinias who were already grouped around us. This had come about because Ctesippus had taken a seat a long way from Cleinias, and when Euthydemus leaned forward in talking to me, he apparently obscured Ctesippus' c view of Cleinias, who was sitting between us. So Ctesippus, who wanted to look at his darling, as well as being interested in the discussion, sprang up first and stationed himself right in front of us. When the others saw him doing this, they gathered around too, not only Cleinias' lovers but the followers of Euthydemus and Dionysodorus as well.[12] These were the ones I pointed to d when I told Euthydemus that everyone was ready to learn. Then Ctesippus agreed very eagerly and so did all the rest, and all together they besought the pair to demonstrate the power of their wisdom.

So I said, Euthydemus and Dionysodorus, do your absolute best to gratify these people and give a demonstration—and do it for my sake too. To give a complete one would obviously be a lengthy business; but tell me just this: are you able to make only that man good who is already persuaded that he ought to e take lessons from you, or can you also make the man good who is not yet persuaded on this point, either because he believes that this thing, virtue, cannot be taught at all, or because he thinks that you two are not its teachers? Come tell me, does the task of persuading a man in this frame of mind both that virtue can be taught, and that you are the ones from whom he could learn it best, belong to this same art or to some other one?

It belongs to this same art, Socrates, said Dionysodorus.[13]

12 For a similar scene, see *Lysis* 207A ff. Plato also arranges his characters with care in the *Charmides* (155BC) and *Protagoras* (317D); and, of course, the order of speeches in the *Symposium* is determined by the positions of the banqueters.
13 Dionysodorus' casual assurance that of course the art of eristic can fulfill the necessary conditions is comparable to the attitude of Gorgias when

Then, Dionysodorus, I said, you and your brother are the
275A men of the present day best able to exhort a man to philosophy
and the practice of virtue?
This is exactly what we think, Socrates.

Then put off the rest of your display to another time and
give us a demonstration of this one thing: persuade this young
man here that he ought to love wisdom and have a care for
virtue, and you will oblige both me and all the present company. The boy's situation is this: both I and all these people
want him to become as good as possible. He is the son of Axio-
B chus (son of the old Alcibiades) and is cousin to the present
Alcibiades—his name is Cleinias. He is young, and we are
anxious about him, as one naturally is about a boy of his age,
for fear that somebody might get in ahead of us and turn his
mind to some other interest and ruin him. So you two have
arrived at the best possible moment. If you have no objection,
make trial of the boy and converse with him in our presence.

When I had spoken, in almost these exact words, Euthydemus
answered, with a mixture of bravery and confidence, It makes
C no difference to us, Socrates, so long as the young man is willing
to answer.[14]

As a matter of fact, he is quite used to that, I said, since these
people here are always coming to ask him all sorts of questions
and to converse with him. So he is pretty brave at answering.

As to what happened next, Crito, how shall I give you an
adequate description of it? It is no small task to be able to recall
such wisdom in detail, it was so great. So I ought to begin my
D account as the poets do, by invoking the Muses and Memory.
SCENE I Well, Euthydemus, as I remember, began something like this:

---

he assures Socrates that if a man comes to study rhetoric not knowing good
and evil, he, Gorgias, will of course teach him that too (*Gorgias* 460A). As
we shall see presently, it is dialectic, not eristic, which convinces Cleinias
that virtue (wisdom) can be taught (282C).

14 The sophists have no interest in Cleinias' moral improvement; they
merely desire to obtain a respondent for a demonstration of their eristic
tricks. (There seems to be something similar in the selection of the young
Aristoteles at *Parmenides* 137B. Cf. also *Sophist* 217D.)

Cleinias, which are the men who learn, the wise or the ignorant?[15]

Being confronted with this weighty question, the boy blushed
and looked at me in doubt. And I, seeing that he was troubled,
said, Cheer up, Cleinias, and choose bravely whichever seems
to you to be the right answer—he may be doing you a very great   275E
service.

Just at this moment Dionysodorus leaned a little toward me
and, smiling all over his face, whispered in my ear and said, I
may tell you beforehand, Socrates, that whichever way the boy
answers he will be refuted.

While he was saying this, Cleinias gave his answer, so that I
had no chance to advise the boy to be careful; and he answered   276A
that the wise were the learners.

Then Euthydemus said, Are there some whom you call teachers, or not?

He agreed that there were.

And the teachers are teachers of those who learn, I suppose,
in the same way that the music master and the writing master
were teachers of you and the other boys when you were pupils?

He agreed.

And when you were learning, you did not yet know the things
you were learning, did you?

No, he said.

And were you wise when you did not know these things?   B

By no means, he said.

Then if not wise, ignorant?

---

[15] Euthydemus' first question to Cleinias introduces a connected group of
four arguments employing equivocal terms in such a way as to produce, in
each case, not a real but an apparent refutation. (An apparent refutation
is precisely what Aristotle identifies with a sophistical refutation; see his
book on the fallacies, On Sophistical Refutations 164a20 ff.) The terms
chosen for the purpose ("wise," "know," "learn," and their opposites) seem
to have been notoriously productive of fallacious arguments. See, for instance, Meno 80DE for the argument about the impossibility of knowledge,
and Theaetetus 199A for a reference to "dragging 'know' and 'learn' this
way and that"; and Aristotle, Metaphysics 1049b33 for a "sophistical refutation" about learning.

Very much so.

Then in the process of learning what you did not know, you learned while you were ignorant?

The boy nodded.

Then it is the ignorant who learn, Cleinias, and not the wise, as you suppose.[16]

When he said this, the followers of Dionysodorus and Euthydemus broke into applause and laughter, just like a chorus at a sign from their director. And before the boy could well recover his breath, Dionysodorus took up the argument and said, Well then, Cleinias, when the writing master gave you dictation, which of the boys learned the piece, the wise or the ignorant?

The wise, said Cleinias.

276c

16 This argument and the next are a pair and should be considered together. First to be noted is that Euthydemus' original question (275D) was posed in terms of contradictories; Cleinias was offered no middle ground between the wise and the ignorant. This procedure is standard eristic practice, as we shall see. The key to the refutation is given by Plato himself in Socrates' speech beginning at 277D where Socrates explains to Cleinias that the word *manthanein* (usually translated "learn") can mean not only to get information about some matter, but also to use information already possessed to inspect the same matter (to understand, *sunienai*, or, in a sense, recognize, what is previously known). Thus it is possible to apply the same word "to both the man who knows and the man who does not" (278A). The equivocation becomes clear if the argument is set out as follows:

Those who understand are those who know. (The learners are the wise.)
When Cleinias got information about music, he was not knowing about it.
Those who get information are the not knowing. (The learners are the ignorant.)

Alternatively, it would be possible to analyze the argument in terms of another ambiguity not mentioned by Plato but pointed out by most commentators, that which is present in the terms "wise" and "ignorant," which can mean either (a) intelligent and stupid, or (b) informed and uninformed. The same argument could then be interpreted as:

Those who get information are the intelligent. (The learners are the wise.)
When Cleinias got information about music, he was uninformed about it.
Those who get information are the not knowing. (The learners are the ignorant.)

In neither formulation does a real refutation take place, since in the first case the sense of *manthanein* has changed, and, in the second, that of "wise" (*sophos*).

Then it is the wise who learn, and not the ignorant, and you gave Euthydemus a wrong answer just now.[17]

Whereupon the supporters of the pair laughed and cheered 276D very loudly indeed, in admiration of their cleverness. We, on the other hand, were panic-struck and kept quiet. Euthydemus, observing our distress, and in order to confound us further, would not let the boy go but went on questioning him and, like a skillful dancer, gave a double twist to his questions on the same point, saying, Do those who learn learn the things they know or the things they do not know?

And Dionysodorus again whispered to me in a low voice, This is another, Socrates, just like the first. E

Mercy on us, I said, the first question certainly seemed good enough!

All our questions are of this same inescapable sort, Socrates, he said.

And this, no doubt, is the reason why your pupils admire you so much, I said.

Just then Cleinias answered Euthydemus that the learners learned what they do not know, whereupon Euthydemus put him through the same course of questions as before.

What then, he said, don't you know your letters?[18] 277A

17 At 275E Dionysodorus whispered to Socrates that Cleinias would be refuted no matter which way he answered the question at 275D; in other words, he and Euthydemus had in readiness arguments designed to refute either answer. The present procedure is to take the conclusion of the first argument as the thesis for a companion argument; that is, we now have the refutation which would have been produced if Cleinias had originally answered "the ignorant," instead of "the wise." Again the refutation is brought off by means of an equivocation. In the conclusion of (1) and in the thesis of (2) we have *manthanein* in the sense of "get information"; in the question about the writing master, the sense has been shifted to "understand." (Or, as before, an analysis could also be made in terms of uninformed and intelligent; see above, note 16.)

18 The following passage is one of several which tell against Ryle's view that Plato's use of the model of letters should be construed in phonetic terms. See Gilbert Ryle, "Letters and Syllables in Plato," *Philosophical Review*, LXIX (1960), 431–451; and, in answer to Ryle, David Gallop, "Plato and the Alphabet," *Philosophical Review*, LXXII (1963), 364–376, esp. 364–365.

Yes, he said.

Then you know them all?

He agreed.

Whenever anyone dictates anything, doesn't he dictate letters?

He agreed.

Then doesn't he dictate something you know, if you really
277B know them all?

He agreed to this too.

Well then, he said, you are not the one who learns what
someone dictates, are you, but the one who doesn't know his
letters is the one who learns?

No, he said, I am the one who learns.

Then you learn what you know, he said, if you in fact do
know all your letters.

He agreed.

Then your answer was wrong, he said.[19]

Euthydemus had barely said this when Dionysodorus picked
up the argument as though it were a ball and aimed it at the
boy again, saying, Euthydemus is completely deceiving you,
Cleinias. Tell me, isn't learning the acquisition of the knowledge of what one learns?

Cleinias agreed.

And what about knowing? he said. Is it anything except having knowledge already?

[19] Dionysodorus whispers to Socrates at 276E that "this is another [ques-
tion] just like the first," and Socrates in his analysis says that "there was
something similar to this in the second question, when they asked you
whether people learn what they know or what they do not know" (278AB).
Thus we may suppose that Euthydemus and Dionysodorus again have refutations ready for either answer, and that the two senses of "learn" will
again be operative. Cleinias' choice of answer shows that he takes *manthanein* in the sense of "get information," so the sophists select an object of
manthanein for which the sense "understand" is more appropriate. The
fallacy of composition is also involved, for although Cleinias may know each
letter of the alphabet individually, he does not necessarily know every word
that is composed of these letters. The use of this fallacy has the effect of
shifting the sense of "know" from "recognize" to something like "compre-
hend." Aristotle appears to be thinking of this passage at *Rhetoric*
1401a29 ff.

He agreed. 277C

Then not knowing is not yet having knowledge?

He agreed with him.

And are those who acquire something those who have it already or those who do not?

Those who do not.

And you have admitted, haven't you, that those who do not know belong to the group of those who do not have something?

He nodded.

Then the learners belong to those who acquire and not to those who have?

He agreed.

Then it is those who do not know who learn, Cleinias, and not those who know.[20]

Euthydemus was hastening to throw the young man for the D third fall when I, seeing that he was going down and wanting to give him a chance to breathe so that he should not turn coward and disgrace us, encouraged him, saying, Don't be surprised, Cleinias, if these arguments seem strange to you, since perhaps you don't take in what the visitors are doing with you. They are doing exactly what people do in the Corybantic mysteries when they enthrone a person they intend to initiate.[21] If you have been initiated you know that there is dancing and

[20] The connection between arguments (3) and (4) is by no means as clear as that between (1) and (2): whereas the emphasis in (3) was on the object of *manthanein*, in (4) it has shifted to a definition of *manthanein* that is independent of its object. But Dionysodorus' remark, "Euthydemus is completely deceiving you, Cleinias" (277B), seems to imply that the new argument (4) will refute the conclusion of the previous argument (3). Nor are we given a fresh thesis to be refuted; it must be supplied either from the conclusion of (3), in which case it would be "those who learn learn what they know," or, more probably, from the conclusion of (4), in which case it would be "those who know learn." (I would hazard a guess that Plato would regard these two statements as roughly equivalent: a man who learns what he knows is a knower, so that it is a knower who learns.) In the argument itself the original sense of *manthanein* (assuming that I have supplied the correct thesis) seems to be "understand," whereas later the sense is clearly the more usual one of "getting information."

[21] The Corybantes were attendants on the Phrygian goddess Cybele.

sport on these occasions; and now these two are doing nothing
277E except dancing around you and making sportive leaps with a
view to initiating you presently. So you must now imagine yourself to be hearing the first part of the sophistic mysteries. In the
first place, as Prodicus[22] says, you must learn about the correct
use of words; and our two visitors are pointing out this very
thing, that you did not realize that people use the word "learn"
not only in the situation in which a person who has no knowl-
278A edge of a thing in the beginning acquires it later, but also when
he who has this knowledge already uses it to inspect the same
thing, whether this is something spoken or something done. (As
a matter of fact, people call the latter "understand" rather than
"learn," but they do sometimes call it "learn" as well.) Now
this, as they are pointing out, had escaped your notice—that
the same word is applied to opposite sorts of men, to both the
man who knows and the man who does not. There was something similar to this in the second question, when they asked
B you whether people learn what they know or what they do not
know. These things are the frivolous part of study (which is why
I also tell you that the men are jesting); and I call these things
"frivolity" because even if a man were to learn many or even
all such things, he would be none the wiser as to how matters
stand but would only be able to make fun of people, tripping
them up and overturning them by means of the distinctions in
words, just like the people who pull the chair out from under
a man who is going to sit down and then laugh gleefully when
C they see him sprawling on his back. So you must think of their
performance as having been mere play. But after this they will
doubtless show you serious things, if anyone will, and I shall give
them a lead to make sure they hand over what they promised
me. They said they would give a demonstration of hortatory
skill, but now it seems to me that they must have thought it
necessary to make fun of you before beginning. So, Euthydemus

---

22 The sophist Prodicus of Ceos is usually associated by Plato with nice
distinctions in the meanings of words. See especially the parody of his style
at *Protagoras* 337AC, and briefer references at *Charmides* 163D, *Protagoras*
358AB, and *Cratylus* 384B.

and Dionysodorus, put an end to this joking; I think we have   278D
had enough of it. The next thing to do is to give an exhibition
of persuading the young man that he ought to devote himself to
wisdom and virtue. But first I shall give you two a demonstration of the way in which I conceive the undertaking and of the
sort of thing I want to hear. And if I seem to you to be doing
this in an unprofessional and ridiculous way, don't laugh at me
—it is out of a desire to hear your wisdom that I have the
audacity to improvise in front of you. Therefore, you and your
disciples restrain yourselves and listen without laughing; and   E
you, son of Axiochus, answer me:

Do all men wish to do well?[23] Or is this question one of the   SCENE II
ridiculous ones I was afraid of just now? I suppose it is stupid
even to raise such a question, since there could hardly be a man
who would not wish to do well.

No, there is no such person, said Cleinias.

Well then, I said, the next question is, since we wish to do
well, how are we to do so? Would it be through having many
good things? Or is this question still more simple-minded than
the other, since this must obviously be the case too?

He agreed.

Well then, what kinds of existing things are good for us? Or   279A
perhaps this isn't a difficult question and we don't need an important personage to supply the answer because everybody
would tell us that to be rich is a good—isn't that so?

Very much so, he said.

And so with being healthy, and handsome, and having a sufficient supply of the other things the body needs?   B

He agreed.

And, again, it is clear that noble birth, and power, and honor
in one's country are goods.

---

23 The Greek expression *eu prattein* can mean "do well" not only in the
sense of "prosper" (and be happy), but also in the sense of "do right." (Cf.
Republic X, 621D, where the choice of *eu prattōmen* as the last words of the
dialogue seems to indicate Plato's consciousness of this double sense, and
Charmides 172A.) The ambiguity does not, however, affect the validity of
the argument, as was the case with the equivocal terms employed by the
sophists in Scene I.

He agreed.

Then which goods do we have left? I said. What about being self-controlled and just and brave? For heaven's sake tell me, Cleinias, whether you think we will be putting these in the right place if we class them as goods or if we refuse to do so? Perhaps someone might quarrel with us on this point—how does it seem to you?

They are goods, said Cleinias.

279C   Very well, said I. And where in the company shall we station wisdom? Among the goods, or what shall we do with it?

Among the goods.

Now be sure we do not leave out any goods worth mentioning.

I don't think we are leaving out any, said Cleinias.

But I remembered one and said, Good heavens, Cleinias, we are in danger of leaving out the greatest good of all!

Which one is that? he said.

Good fortune, Cleinias, which everybody, even quite worthless people, says is the greatest of the goods.

You are right, he said.

And I reconsidered a second time and said, son of Axiochus,

D   you and I have nearly made ourselves ridiculous in front of our visitors.

How so? he said.

Because in putting good fortune in our previous list we are now saying the same thing all over again.

What do you mean?

Surely it is ridiculous, when a thing has already been brought up, to bring it up again and say the same things twice.

What do you mean by that?

Wisdom is surely good fortune, I said—this is something even a child would know.

He was amazed—he is still so young and simple-minded.

E   I noticed his surprise and said, You know, don't you, Cleinias, that flute players have the best luck when it comes to success in flute music?

He agreed.

And the writing masters at reading and writing?

Certainly.

What about the perils of the sea—surely you don't think that, as a general rule, any pilots have better luck than the wise ones?

Certainly not.

And again, if you were on a campaign, with which general would you prefer to share both the danger and the luck, a wise one or an ignorant one? 280A

With a wise one.

And if you were sick, would you rather take a chance with a wise doctor or with an ignorant one?

With a wise one.

Then it is your opinion, I said, that it is luckier to do things in the company of wise men than ignorant ones?

He agreed.

So wisdom makes men fortunate in every case, since I don't suppose she would ever make any sort of mistake but must necessarily do right and be lucky—otherwise she would no longer be wisdom.[24]

We finally agreed (I don't know quite how) that, in sum, the situation was this: if a man had wisdom, he had no need of any good fortune in addition. When we had settled this point, I went back and asked him how our former statements might be affected. We decided, I said, that if we had many good things, we should be happy and do well. B

He agreed.

And would the possession of good things make us happy if they were of no advantage to us, or if they were of some? C

If they were of some advantage, he said.

And would they be advantageous to us if we simply had them and did not use them? For instance, if we had a great deal of food but didn't eat any, or plenty to drink but didn't drink any, would we derive any advantage from these things?

Certainly not, he said.

[24] John Gould, in his *The Development of Plato's Ethics* (Cambridge, 1955), p. 27, has some interesting remarks on this passage as an example of an analytic proposition typical of the Socratic ethics.

Well then, if every workman had all the materials necessary for his particular job but never used them, would he do well by reason of possessing all the things a workman requires? For instance, if a carpenter were provided with all his tools and plenty of wood but never did any carpentry, could he be said to benefit

280D from their possession?

Not at all, he said.

Well then, if a man had money and all the good things we were mentioning just now but made no use of them, would he be happy as a result of having these good things?

Clearly not, Socrates.

So it seems, I said, that the man who means to be happy must not only have such goods but must use them too, or else there is no advantage in having them.

You are right.

Then are these two things, the possession of good things and

E the use of them, enough to make a man happy, Cleinias?

They seem so to me, at any rate.

If, I said, he uses them rightly, or if he does not?

If he uses them rightly.

Well spoken, I said. Now I suppose there is more harm done if someone uses a thing wrongly than if he lets it alone—in the first instance there is evil, but in the second neither evil nor

281A good. Or isn't this what we maintain?

He agreed that it was.

Then what comes next? In working and using wood there is surely nothing else that brings about right use except the knowledge of carpentry, is there?

Certainly not.

And, again, I suppose that in making utensils, it is knowledge that produces the right method.

He agreed.

And also, I said, with regard to using the goods we mentioned first—wealth and health and beauty—was it knowledge that

B ruled and directed our conduct in relation to the right use of all such things as these, or some other thing?

It was knowledge, he said.

Then knowledge seems to provide men not only with good fortune but also with well-doing, in every case of possession or action.

He agreed.

Then in heaven's name, I said, is there any advantage in other possessions without good sense and wisdom? Would a man with no sense profit more if he possessed and did much or if he possessed and did little?[25] Look at it this way: if he did less, would he not make fewer mistakes; and if he made fewer mis-   281C takes, would he not do less badly;[26] and if he did less badly, would he not be less miserable?

Yes, indeed, he said.

And in which case would one do less, if one were poor or if one were rich?

Poor, he said.

And if one were weak or strong?

Weak.

If one were held in honor or in dishonor?

In dishonor.

And if one were brave and self-controlled would one do less, or if one were a coward?

A coward.

Then the same would be true if one were lazy rather than industrious?

He agreed.

And slow rather than quick, and dull of sight and hearing   D rather than keen?

We agreed with each other on all points of this sort.

So, to sum up, Cleinias, I said, it seems likely that with respect to all the things we called good in the beginning, the correct account is not that in themselves they are good by nature, but rather as follows: if ignorance controls them, they are greater evils than their opposites, to the extent that they are more

25 Omitting νοῦν ἔχων with Iamblichus.

26 kakōs prattein is ambiguous here in the same way as eu prattein at 278E; that is, it means both "fare badly" and "do harm." (The rather awkward expression "do less badly" is intended to bring this out.)

capable of complying with a bad master; but if good sense and wisdom are in control, they are greater goods. In themselves, however, neither sort is of any value.[27]

281E

It seems, he said, to be just as you say.

Then what is the result of our conversation? Isn't it that, of the other things, no one of them is either good or bad, but of these two, wisdom is good and ignorance bad?

He agreed.

282A

Then let us consider what follows: since we all wish to be happy, and since we appear to become so by using things and using them rightly, and since knowledge was the source of rightness and good fortune, it seems to be necessary that every man should prepare himself by every means to become as wise as possible—or isn't this the case?

Yes, it is, he said.

And for a man who thinks he ought to get this from his father much more than money, and not only from his father but also

B

from his guardians and friends (especially those of his city and elsewhere who claim to be his lovers), and who begs and beseeches them to give him some wisdom, there is nothing shameful, Cleinias, nor disgraceful if, for the sake of this, he should become the servant or the slave of a lover or of any man, being willing to perform any honorable service in his desire to become wise.[28] Or don't you think so? I said.

You seem to me to be absolutely right, said he.

C

But only if wisdom can be taught, Cleinias, I said, and does not come to men of its own accord. This point still remains for us to investigate and is not yet settled between you and me.

As far as I am concerned, Socrates, he said, I think it can be taught.

I was pleased and said, I like the way you talk, my fine fellow,

---

27 Plato is making a point related to that in the *Laches* 195c about the inability of the doctor qua doctor to tell whether health really is good for his patient. Cf. also *Gorgias* 511c ff. for the pilot who cannot tell whether or not he has benefited his passengers by saving them from drowning.

28 A similar view is expressed at *Symposium* 184c: "there remains one sort of voluntary slavery which is not disgraceful, the slavery to virtue."

and you have done me a good turn by relieving me of a long investigation of this very point, whether or not wisdom can be taught.[29] Now then, since you believe both that it can be taught and that it is the only existing thing which makes a man happy and fortunate, surely you would agree that it is necessary to love 282D wisdom and you mean to do this yourself.

This is just what I mean to do, Socrates, as well as ever I can.

When I heard this I was delighted and said, There, Dionysodorus and Euthydemus, is my example of what I want a hortatory argument[30] to be, though amateurish, perhaps, and expressed at length and with some difficulty. Now let either of you who wishes give us a demonstration of the same thing in a professional manner. Or if you do not wish to do that, then start where I left off and show the boy what follows next: E whether he ought to acquire every sort of knowledge, or whether there is one sort that he ought to get in order to be a happy man and a good one, and what it is. As I said in the beginning, it is of great importance to us that this young man should become wise and good.

This is what I said, Crito, and I paid particular attention to 283A what should come next and watched to see just how they would pick up the argument and where they would start persuading the young man to practice wisdom and virtue. The elder of the two, Dionysodorus, took up the argument first and we all gazed

[29] This passage really does nothing to settle the question whether the *Euthydemus* precedes or follows the *Meno*, although attempts have been made to use it in this connection. See the discussion by R. S. Bluck, *Plato's 'Meno'* (Cambridge, 1961), pp. 113–114.

[30] According to I. Düring (*Aristotle's 'Protrepticus': An Attempt at Reconstruction* [Göteborg, 1961], p. 19), this passage (278E–282D) is "the earliest example of a typical protreptic preseved to us." It has long been recognized that parts of Iamblichus' *Protrepticus* (Pistelli 24.24–27.10) are based on this passage and on the second protreptic passage (288D–293A). See W. G. Rabinowitz (*Aristotle's 'Protrepticus' and the Sources of Its Reconstruction* [Berkeley, 1957], pp. 55–57) for a discussion of Iamblichus' methods of summary. (Contrary to the main tradition, Rabinowitz thinks it unnecessary to postulate the *Protrepticus* of Aristotle as an intervening source. For criticism of this view, see Philip Merlan, *From Platonism to Neo-Platonism* [2nd ed. rev.; The Hague, 1960], pp. 155–159.)

at him in expectation of hearing some wonderful words immediately. And this is just what happened, since the man began an
283B argument which was certainly wonderful, in a way, Crito, and
worth your while to hear, since it was an incitement to virtue.

SCENE III Tell me, Socrates, he said, and all you others who say you want
this young man to become wise—are you saying this as a joke
or do you want it truly and in earnest?

This gave me the idea that they must have thought we were
joking earlier when we asked them to talk to the boy, and that
this was why they made a joke of it and failed to take it seriously.

c When this idea occurred to me, I insisted all the more that we
were in dead earnest.

And Dionysodorus said, Well, take care, Socrates, that you
don't find yourself denying these words.

I have given thought to the matter, I said, and I shall never
come to deny them.

Well then, he said, you say you want him to become wise?

Very much so.

And at the present moment, he said, is Cleinias wise or not?

He says he is not yet, at least—he is a modest person, I said.

D But you people wish him to become wise, he said, and not to
be ignorant?

We agreed.

Therefore, you wish him to become what he is not, and no
longer to be what he is now?

When I heard this I was thrown into confusion, and he broke
in upon me while I was in this state and said, Then since you
wish him no longer to be what he is now,[31] you apparently wish
for nothing else but his death. Such friends and lovers must be

---

[31] The Greek order is "you wish him, what he is now, no longer to be."
With the emphasis thrown onto the last phrase, the sense of "to be" shifts
easily from copulative to existential, from "to be ignorant" to "to exist." See
A. L. Peck, "Plato and the ΜΕΓΙΣΤΑ ΓΕΝΗ of the Sophist," Classical
Quarterly, New Series, II (1952), 47, for some remarks on this argument;
and, for a more general discussion of the various senses of einai, see John
Ackrill, "Plato and the Copula: Sophist 251–259," Journal of Hellenic
Studies, LXXVII, Pt. I (1957), 1–6. But see also W. G. Runciman, Plato's
Later Epistemology (Cambridge, 1962), p. 63, and passim on the copula.

worth a lot who desire above all things that their beloved should
utterly perish!

When Ctesippus heard this he became angry on his favorite's   283E
account and said, Thurian stranger, if it were not a rather rude
remark, I would say "perish yourself" for taking it into your
head to tell such a lie about me and the rest, which I think is a
wicked thing to say—that I could wish this person to die!

Why Ctesippus, said Euthydemus, do you think it possible to
tell lies?

Good heavens yes, he said, I should be raving if I didn't.

When one speaks the thing one is talking about, or when one
does not speak it?[32]

When one speaks it, he said.   284A

So that if he speaks this thing, he speaks no other one of
things that are except the very one he speaks?

Of course, said Ctesippus.

And the thing he speaks is one of those that are, distinct from
the rest?

Certainly.

Then the person speaking that thing speaks what is, he said.

Yes.

But surely the person who speaks what is and things that are
speaks the truth—so that Dionysodorus, if he speaks things that
are, speaks the truth and tells no lies about you.

Yes, said Ctesippus, but a person who speaks these things,   B
Euthydemus, does not speak things that are.

32 The translation throughout this next argument employs some admit-
tedly awkward expressions. For "speak a thing" (legein ti) "mention" or
"utter" would be more accurate but would not pave the way so well for
"speak the truth." "Things that are" is also not idiomatic English, but
seemed necessary in view of the subsequent shift to "things that are the
case (i.e., true)." (Cf. R. S. Bluck, "False Statement in the Sophist," Journal
of Hellenic Studies, LXXVII, Pt. II (1957), 184: "The fallacy lies in the
ambiguity of τὸ ὄν (or τὰ ὄντα) which can refer either (i) to an existing
person or thing or (ii) to truth.") Certainly the mechanics of the fallacy are
obscured if this phrase ta onta is altered to "the facts" as has been done by
P. G. Rouse in revising W. H. D. Rouse's translation (Plato: The Collected
Dialogues, ed. Edith Hamilton and Huntington Cairns [New York, 1961]. See
p. 420n.)

And Euthydemus said, But the things that are not surely do not exist, do they?[33]

No, they do not exist.

Then there is nowhere that the things that are not are?

Nowhere.

Then there is no possibility that any person whatsoever could do anything to the things that are not so as to make them be[34] when they are nowhere?

It seems unlikely to me, said Ctesippus.

Well then, when the orators speak to the people, do they do nothing?

No, they do something, he said.

284c Then if they do something, they also make something?

Yes.

Speaking, then, is doing and making?

He agreed.

Then nobody speaks things that are not, since he would then be making something, and you have admitted that no one is capable of making something that is not. So according to your own statement, nobody tells lies; but if Dionysodorus really does speak, he speaks the truth and things that are.[35]

33 The transition is easier here if we assume that Euthydemus is distorting Ctesippus' previous phrase "does not speak things that are" into "speaks things that are not," that is, that he twists *ou ta onta legei* into *ta mē onta legei*. See H. Cherniss, "*Timaeus* 38A8–B5," *Journal of Hellenic Studies*, LXXVII Pt. I (1957), 19.

34 Reading ὥστε καὶ εἶναι with Hermann. (The emendation is discussed by E. H. Gifford in his edition [Oxford, 1905] but is not recorded by Burnet.)

35 The argument is discussed by I. M. Crombie, *Plato: The Midwife's Apprentice* (London, 1963), pp. 112–113: "How did we get into this tangle? In something like the following way. 'Report', and certain other verbs of *saying* such as 'mention' or 'recount', can govern either a direct object or a *that*-clause. (Plato shows his awareness of this by the tricks he plays with *legein* in *Euthydemus* 283–284.) In the direct-object construction what is reported is a constituent of the world, existent or non-existent; in the other construction what is reported is a proposition, true or false. The temptation to say that when I make a false statement I say nothing arises from confusing the two objects. . . . It is in fact by leaving the proposition out of the analysis, and concentrating on the situation, that the trouble arises." (See also a longer discussion of this general type of argument by the same author

Yes indeed, Euthydemus, said Ctesippus, but he speaks things
that are only in a certain way and not as really is the case.
What do you mean, Ctesippus? said Dionysodorus. Are there
some persons who speak of things as they are?   284D
There certainly are, he said—gentlemen and those who speak
the truth.
Now then, he said, are not good things well and bad things ill?
He agreed.
And you admit that gentlemen speak of things as they are?
Yes, I do.
Then good men speak ill of bad things, Ctesippus, if they do
in fact speak of them as they are.[36]
They certainly do, he said—at any rate they speak ill of bad

---

under the heading "The Paradox of False Belief" in *An Examination of
Plato's Doctrines* [London, 1963], II, 486 ff.) An additional complication is
provided by the fact that the Greek verb *poiein* means not only "do," like
prattein, but also "make" or "create." This makes it natural to suppose that
any sort of activity results in an object (as at 284C1) and thus to question
the existential status of such objects. Cf. Shakespeare, *As You Like It*, I.i.26:
"*Oliver:* Now sir! what make you here? *Orlando:* Nothing; I am not taught
to make anything."

[36] Again the English must necessarily be awkward if the argument is to be
made at all clear, and even so some expansion may be helpful. Ctesippus, still
smarting from the affront to his favorite at 283D, has objected that although
the sophists may speak of things that are, they do not speak of them *as*
they are; they do not speak the truth, in other words. Those who do speak
the truth are the *kaloi kagathoi*, gentlemen or *good men*. (The implication
is that the sophists are not gentlemen.) Now it is the part of a Greek gentleman to speak well. The sophists construct their argument by combining
this (unspoken) assumption with Ctesippus' stipulation that gentlemen
must speak of things as they are. Their way of interpreting how "things
are" is to introduce, in each case, the adverb suggested by the adjective: good
things are spoken of as they are if they are spoken of well, bad things badly,
and so forth. The conclusion, that good men speak ill of bad things, thus
has two distasteful implications, one that the good should speak injuriously
of anything, even something bad, and the other that a gentleman could be
a poor speaker. The latter notion, which is probably dominant, occurs in a
neat form in Diogenes Laertius, II. 35: Socrates, on being told that someone
spoke ill of him (*kakōs legein*), replied that the person in question had never
learned to speak well (be a good speaker).

men. If you take my advice you will take care not to be one of
them in case the good speak ill of *you*. For rest assured that the
good speak ill of the bad.

And do they speak greatly of the great and hotly of the hot?
asked Euthydemus.

Very much so, said Ctesippus, and what is more, they speak
coldly of persons who argue in a frigid fashion.[37]

You, Ctesippus, said Dionysodorus, are being abusive, very
abusive indeed.

I am certainly doing no such thing, Dionysodorus, he said,
since I like you. I am merely giving you a piece of friendly advice
and endeavoring to persuade you never to say, so rudely and to
my face, that I want my most cherished friends to die.

Since they seemed to be getting pretty rough with each other,
I started to joke with Ctesippus and said, Ctesippus, I think we
ought to accept what the strangers tell us, if they are willing to
be generous, and not to quarrel over a word. If they really know
how to destroy men so as to make good and sensible people out
of bad and stupid ones, and the two of them have either found
out for themselves or learned from someone else a kind of ruin
or destruction by which they do away with a bad man and
render him good, if, as I say, they know how to do this—well,
they clearly do, since they specifically claimed that the art they
had recently discovered was that of making good men out of
bad ones—then let us concede them the point and permit them
to destroy the boy for us and make him wise—and do the same
to the rest of us as well. And if you young men are afraid, let
them "try it on the Carian,"[38] as they say, and I will be the
victim. Being elderly, I am ready to run the risk, and I surrender
myself to Dionysodorus here just as I might to Medea of Col-

37 Literally, "they speak coldly of cold persons and say they argue coldly."

38 Dr. A. M. Snodgrass writes me that he thinks the Carians in question
are more likely to be Carian mercenaries than Carian slaves. Aside from the
fact that Carian mercenaries seem to have been famous (see Herodotus, V.
111–112), he points out that to lose a slave, even a bad one, would be to lose
something of value, whereas to lose a mercenary means that it will no longer
be necessary to pay him. In any case, the force of the expression is clear: try
it on the dog or on a guinea pig. Cf. also *Laches* 187B.

chis.[39] Let him destroy me, or if he likes, boil me, or do whatever else he wants, but he must make me good.

And Ctesippus said, I too, Socrates, am ready to hand myself over to the visitors; and I give them permission to skin me even more thoroughly than they are doing now so long as my hide will in the end become not a wineskin (which is what happened to Marsyas),[40] but a piece of virtue. And yet Dionysodorus here 285D thinks I am cross with him. It's not that I'm cross—I'm simply contradicting the things he said which I find objectionable. So, my fine Dionysodorus, don't call contradiction abuse—abuse is something quite different.

And Dionysodorus answered, Are you making your speech on the assumption that there exists such a thing as contradiction, Ctesippus?

I certainly am, he said, decidedly so. And do you think there E is none, Dionysodorus?

Well you, at any rate could not prove that you have ever heard one person contradicting another.

Do you really mean that? he answered. Well then, just listen to Ctesippus contradicting Dionysodorus, if you want to hear my proof.[41]

And do you undertake to back that up?

I certainly do, he said.

Well then, he went on, are there words to describe each thing that exists?

Certainly.

And do they describe it as it is or as it is not?

As it is.

Now if you remember, Ctesippus, he said, we showed a mo- 286A ment ago that no one speaks of things as they are not, since it appeared that no one speaks what does not exist.[42]

[39] Medea persuaded the daughters of Pelias to cut up their father and boil him in a cauldron, telling them that in this way they would renew his youth.

[40] Marsyas, a satyr, challenged Apollo to a musical contest. Apollo, having won the contest, flayed his opponent alive. Cf. Herodotus, VII. 26.

[41] Reading ἀκούωμεν νῦν εἰ with T.

[42] The reference is to 284C.

Well, what about it? said Ctesippus. Are you and I contradicting each other any the less?

Now would we be contradicting, he said, if we were both to speak the[43] description of the same thing? I suppose we would be saying the same things in that case.

He agreed.

286B But when neither of us speaks the description of the thing, would we be contradicting then? Or wouldn't it be the case that neither of us had the thing in mind at all?

He agreed to this too.

But when I speak the description of the thing whereas you speak another description of another thing, do we contradict then?[44] Or is it the case that I speak it but that you speak nothing at all? And how would a person who does not speak contradict one who does?[45]

Ctesippus fell silent at this, but I was astonished at the argument and said, How do you mean, Dionysodorus? The fact is

c that I have heard this particular argument from many persons and at many times, and it never ceases to amaze me. The followers of Protagoras made considerable use of it, and so did some still earlier.[46] It always seems to me to have a wonderful

43 Reading $\langle\tau\grave{o}\nu\rangle$ $\tau o\hat{v}$ with Heindorf.

44 Although Dionysodorus has made a pretense of being exhaustive, he has actually omitted the crucial case, the one in which he speaks the description of the thing whereas Ctesippus speaks another of the *same* thing. It is important for his argument that not only the description but also the thing should *not be* (i.e., not be the same as those mentioned by Ctesippus) so that he can assume the nonexistence of both and thus the impossibility of mentioning either.

45 Notice that the person who speaks something different from another person does not, according to the sophist, speak falsely; he simply does not speak. Cf. the passage about the man beating a bronze pot at *Cratylus* 430A.

46 There has been no general agreement as to the identity of "some still earlier"; probably the reference is to Parmenides. That an argument which is Eleatic in origin should be associated with "Protagoras and his followers" may seem strange since Protagoras is consistently linked with Heraclitus by Plato, e.g., at *Theaetetus* 151E and 160D. But in Plato's view Heraclitus and Parmenides fail equally in establishing a criterion of truth. This point is particularly well illustrated in the *Cratylus* in connection with the failure of the two opposing theories of language. Plato has even amused himself

way of upsetting not just other arguments, but itself as well.[47]
But I think I shall learn the truth about it better from you
than from anyone else. The argument amounts to claiming that
there is no such thing as false speaking, doesn't it? And the person speaking must either speak the truth or else not speak?

He agreed.

Now would you say it was impossible to speak what is false,   286D
but possible to think it?

No, thinking it is not possible either, he said.

Then there is absolutely no such thing as false opinion, I said.
There is not, he said.

Then is there no ignorance, nor are there any ignorant men?
Or isn't this just what ignorance would be, if there should be
any—to speak falsely about things?

It certainly would, he said.

And yet there is no such thing, I said.

He said there was not.

Are you making this statement just for the sake of argument,
Dionysodorus—to say something startling—or do you honestly
believe that there is no such thing as an ignorant man?

Your business is to refute me, he said.   E

Well, but is there such a thing as refutation if one accepts
your thesis that nobody speaks falsely?

No, there is not, said Euthydemus.

Then it can't be that Dionysodorus ordered me to refute him
just now, can it? I said.

---

by giving the Eleatic theory to the Heraclitean Cratylus! (See R. K. Sprague,
Plato's Use of Fallacy [London, 1962], p. 54, note 28.) The denial of contradiction is attributed by Aristotle to Antisthenes (*Topics* 104b20 and *Metaphysics* 1024b31 ff.). But Antisthenes seems to have connected the paradox
with his views on predication, and these are not clearly reflected here.

[47] Protagoras' "man is the measure" also upsets itself, as is pointed out by
Plato at *Theaetetus* 171A. See also Diogenes Laertius, III. 35, where the
following anecdote is recounted: Antisthenes invited Plato to come to one
of his lectures, the subject of which was that there is no contradiction. "Then
how do you write about it?" replied Plato. In the *Euthydemus*, however,
Plato seems more interested in the incompatibility of the sophists' position
on false speaking with their claim to teach. (See below 287A.)

How would anyone order a thing which doesn't exist? Are you in the habit of giving such orders?

The reason I've raised the point, Euthydemus, is that I'm rather thickwitted and don't understand these fine clever things. And perhaps I'm about to ask a rather stupid question, but bear with me. Look at it this way: if it is impossible to speak falsely, or to think falsely, or to be ignorant, then there is no possibility of making a mistake when a man does anything? I mean that it is impossible for a man to be mistaken in his actions—or isn't this what you are saying?

Certainly it is, he said.

This is just where my stupid question comes in, I said. If no one of us makes mistakes either in action or in speech or in thought—if this really is the case—what in heaven's name do you two come here to teach? Or didn't you say just now that if anyone wanted to learn virtue, you would impart it best?

Really, Socrates, said Dionysodorus, interrupting, are you such an old Cronos[48] as to bring up now what we said in the beginning? I suppose if I said something last year, you will bring that up now and still be helpless in dealing with the present argument.

Well you see, I said, these arguments are very difficult (as is natural, since they come from wise men) and this last one you mention turns out to be particularly difficult to deal with. Whatever in the world do you mean by the expression "be helpless in dealing with," Dionysodorus? Doesn't it clearly mean that I am unable to refute the argument? Just tell me, what else is the sense of this phrase "I am helpless in dealing with the argument"?

But at least it is not very difficult to deal with *your* phrase,[49] he said, so go ahead and answer.

Before you answer me, Dionysodorus? I said.

48 As the father of Zeus whom Zeus dethroned, Cronos is a symbol of the out-of-date.

49 Retaining τούτῳ τῷ πάνυ χαλεπὸν χρ ῆσθαι, but reading γ'οὔ with Badham. Dionysodorus has thought up an argument based on the ambiguity in the word *noei* ("have sense"), and he wants to use this instead of facing the question about refutation. He gets his way just below at 287D.

You refuse to answer then? he said.

Well, is it fair?

Perfectly fair, he said.

On what principle? I said. Or isn't it clearly on this one, that you have come here on the present occasion as a man who is completely skilled in arguments, and you know when an answer should be given and when it should not? So now you decline to 287D give any answer whatsoever because you realize you ought not to?

You are babbling instead of being concerned about answering, he said. But, my good fellow, follow my instructions and answer, since you admit that I am wise.

I must obey then, I said, and it seems I am forced to do so, since you are in command, so ask away.

Now are the things that have sense those that have soul, or do things without soul have sense too?

It is the ones with soul that have sense.

And do you know any phrase that has soul? he asked.

Heavens no, not I.

Then why did you ask me just now what was the sense of E my phrase?[50]

I suppose, I said, for no other reason than that I made a mistake on account of being so stupid. Or perhaps I did not make a mistake but was right when I spoke as if phrases had sense? Are you saying that I made a mistake or not? Because if I did not make one you will not refute me no matter how wise you are, and you will be "helpless in dealing with the argument." And if I did make one, you said the wrong thing when you claimed it was impossible to make mistakes—and I'm not talking about 288A things you said last year. So, Dionysodorus and Euthydemus, I said, it looks as if this argument has made no progress and still has the old trouble of falling down itself in the process of knocking down others. And your art has not discovered how to prevent this from happening in spite of your wonderful display of precision in words.

[50] The Greek verb carries the additional sense of "intend," thus implying life and purpose.

And Ctesippus said, Your manner of speech is certainly re-
288B markable, O men of Thurii or Chios, or from wherever and
however you like to be styled, because it matters nothing to you
if you talk complete nonsense.

I was worried in case there might be hard words, and started
to pacify Ctesippus once again, saying, Ctesippus, let me say
to you the same things I was just saying to Cleinias, that you
fail to recognize how remarkable the strangers' wisdom is. It's
just that the two of them are unwilling to give us a serious
demonstration, but are putting on conjuring tricks in imitation
c of that Egyptian sophist, Proteus.[51] So let us imitate Menelaus
and refuse to release the pair until they have shown us their
serious side. I really think some splendid thing in them will
appear whenever they begin to be in earnest, so let us beg and
exhort and pray them to make it known. As for me, I think I
ought once again to take the lead and give an indication of
what sort of persons I pray they will show themselves to be.
D Beginning where I left off earlier, I shall do my best to go
through what comes next so as to spur them to action and in
hopes that out of pity and commiseration for my earnest exer-
tions they may be earnest themselves.

SCENE IV   So, Cleinias, I said, remind me where we left off. As far as I
can remember it was just about at the point where we finally
agreed that it was necessary to love wisdom, wasn't it?[52]

Yes, he said.

Now the love of wisdom, or philosophy,[53] is the acquisition
of knowledge, isn't that so? I said.

Yes, he said.

Well, what sort of knowledge would we acquire if we went
E about it in the right way? Isn't the answer simply this, that it
would be one which will benefit us?

---

51 Proteus, a sea deity, refused to assume his proper shape in the hands
of Menelaus until he had transformed himself into a lion, a dragon, a
panther, an enormous pig, into water, and into a tree, as described by Homer
(*Odyssey* IV. 456 ff.). He was then forced to answer Menelaus' questions.
52 At 282D.
53 The word *philosophia* is translated twice.

Certainly, he said.

And would it benefit us in any way if we knew how to go about and discover where in the earth the greatest quantities of gold are buried?

Perhaps, he said.

But earlier,[54] I said, we gave a thorough demonstration of the point that even if all the gold in the world should be ours with no trouble and without digging for it, we should be no better off—no, not even if we knew how to make stones into gold would the knowledge be worth anything. For unless we also   289A
knew how to use the gold, there appeared to be no value in it. Or don't you remember? I said.

Yes, I remember very well, he said.

Nor does there seem to be any value in any other sort of knowledge which knows how to make things, whether money making or medicine or any other such thing, unless it knows how to use what it makes—isn't this the case?

He agreed.

And again, if there exists the knowledge of how to make men immortal, but without the knowledge of how to use this im-   B
mortality, there seems to be no value in it, if we are to conclude anything from what has already been settled.

We agreed on all this.

Then what we need, my fair friend, I said, is a kind of knowledge which combines making and knowing how to use the thing which it makes.

So it appears, he said.

Then it seems not at all needful for us to become lyre makers and skilled in some such knowledge as that. For there the art   C
which makes is one thing and that which uses is another; they are quite distinct although they deal with the same thing. There is a great difference between lyre making and lyre playing, isn't there?

He agreed.

And it is equally obvious that we stand in no need of the art of flute playing, since this is another of the same kind.

54 At 280D, although the point made was more general.

He said yes.

Seriously then, said I, if we were to learn the art of writing speeches, is this the art which we would have to get if we are going to be happy?

I don't think so, said Cleinias in answer.

289D   On what ground do you say this? I asked.

Well, he said, I notice that certain speech writers have no idea of how to use the particular speeches they themselves have written, in the same way that the lyre makers have no idea of how to use their lyres. And in the former case too, there are other people who are capable of using what the speech writers have composed but are themselves unable to write. So it is clear that in regard to speeches too, there is one art of making and another of using.

You seem to me, I said, to have sufficient ground for stating that the art of speech writing is not the one a man would be happy if he acquired. And yet it was in this connection that I expected the very knowledge we have been seeking all this time

E   would put in an appearance. Because, as far as I am concerned, whenever I have any contact with these same men who write speeches, they strike me as being persons of surpassing wisdom, Cleinias; and this art of theirs seems to me something marvellous and lofty. Though after all there is nothing remarkable in this, since it is part of the enchanters' art and but slightly in-

290A   ferior to it. For the enchanters' art consists in charming vipers and spiders and scorpions and other wild things, and in curing diseases, while the other art consists in charming and persuading the members of juries and assemblies and other sorts of crowds. Or do you have some other notion of it? I said.

No, he said, it seems to me to be just as you say.

Where should we turn next, then? I asked. To which one of the arts?

I find myself at a loss, he said.

But I think I have discovered it, said I.

Which one is it? said Cleinias.

B   The art of generalship seems to me, I said, to be the one

which, more than any other, a man would be happy if he acquired.[55]

It doesn't seem so to me, he said.

How is that? said I.

Well, this art is a kind of man hunting.

What then? I said.

No art of actual hunting, he said, extends any further than pursuing and capturing: whenever the hunters catch what they are pursuing they are incapable of using it, but they and the fishermen hand over their prey to the cooks. And again, geometers and astronomers and calculators (who are hunters too, in 290C a way, for none of these make their diagrams; they simply discover those which already exist), since they themselves have no idea of how to use their prey but only how to hunt it, hand over the task of using their discoveries to the dialecticians—at least, those of them do so who are not completely senseless.[56]

Well done, I said, most handsome and clever Cleinias! And is this really the case?

Very much so. And the same is true of the generals, he said. Whenever they capture some city, or a camp, they hand it over D to the statesmen—for they themselves have no idea of how to use the things they have captured—just in the same way, I imagine, that quail hunters hand theirs over to quail keepers. So, he said, if we are in need of that art which will itself know how to use what it acquires through making or capturing, and if it is an art of this sort which will make us happy, then, he said, we must look for some other art besides that of generalship.

Crito. What do you mean, Socrates? Did that boy utter all E this?

Socrates. You're not convinced of it, Crito?

55 The group of arts about to be discussed differs from the group mentioned above at 289C only in that the object is now something caught or discovered rather than something produced. Cf. the productive and acquisitive arts of *Sophist* 219AD.

56 I would agree with R. Robinson, *Plato's Earlier Dialectic* (2nd ed.; Oxford, 1953), p. 74, that it is "hard to imagine what sort of activity Plato would have classified as a dialectician's use of a mathematical discovery."

Crito. Good heavens no! Because, in my opinion, if he spoke like that, he needs no education, either from Euthydemus or anyone else.

Socrates. Dear me, then perhaps after all it was Ctesippus who said this, and I am getting absent-minded.

291A *Crito.* Not my idea of Ctesippus!

Socrates. But I'm sure of one thing at least, that it was neither Euthydemus nor Dionysodorus who said it. Do you suppose, my good Crito, that some superior being was there and uttered these things—because I am positive I heard them.

Crito. Yes, by heaven, Socrates, I certainly think it was some superior being, very much so.[57] But after this did you still go on looking for the art? And did you find the one you were looking for or not?

B *Socrates.* Find it, my dear man—I should think not! We were really quite ridiculous—just like children running after crested larks; we kept thinking we were about to catch each one of the knowledges, but they always got away. So why should I recount the whole story? When we got to the kingly art and were giving it a thorough inspection to see whether it might be the one which both provided and created happiness, just there we got into a sort of labyrinth: when we thought we had come to the end, we turned round again and reappeared practically at the

C beginning of our search in just as much trouble as when we started out.

Crito. And how did this come about, Socrates?

Socrates. I shall tell you. We had the idea that the statesman's art and the kingly art were the same.

Crito. And then what?

Socrates. It was due to this art that generalship and the others handed over the management of the products of which they themselves were the craftsmen, as if this art alone knew how to use them. It seemed clear to us that this was the art we were

---

[57] Crito means Socrates himself. Cleinias' remarks and Crito's comments on them contribute, of course, to the contrast between dialectic and eristic which is a keynote of the entire dialogue.

looking for, and that it was the cause of right action in the state, and, to use the language of Aeschylus, that this art alone 291D sits at the helm of the state, governing all things, ruling all things, and making all things useful.[58]

Crito. And wasn't your idea a good one, Socrates?[59]

Socrates. You will form an opinion, Crito, if you like to hear what happened to us next. We took up the question once again in somewhat this fashion: Well, does the kingly art, which rules everything, produce some result for us, or not?[60] Certainly it E does, we said to each other. Wouldn't you say so too, Crito?

Crito. Yes, I would.

Socrates. Then what would you say its result was? For instance, if I should ask you what result does medicine produce, when it rules over all the things in its control, would you not say that this result was health?

Crito. Yes, I would.

Socrates. And what about your own art of farming, when it rules over all the things in its control—what result[61] does it 292A produce? Wouldn't you say that it provides us with nourishment from the earth?

Crito. Yes, I would.

Socrates. Now what about the kingly art; when it rules over all the things in its control—what does it produce? Perhaps you won't find the answer quite so easy in this case.

Crito. No, I certainly don't, Socrates.

Socrates. Nor did we, Crito. But you are aware of this point at least, that if this is to be the art we are looking for, it must be something useful.

[58] The reference is probably to *Seven Against Thebes*, 2.: "whoever, at the helm of the state, handles the tiller with an eye upon affairs. . . ."

[59] Reading οὔκουν as suggested by J. D. Denniston, *The Greek Particles* (2nd ed.; London, 1954), p. 432.

[60] As soon as Socrates begins to inquire whether a master art has a product, we may expect a paradox; see below 292DE. The difficulty is one which is closely tied to the *techne*-analogy. (See the undiscovered subject matter of the rhapsode's art in the *Ion* 539E ff.)

[61] Retaining ἔργον with BW.

Crito. Yes indeed.

Socrates. And it certainly must provide us with something good?

Crito. Necessarily, Socrates.

292B   *Socrates.* And Cleinias and I of course agreed that nothing is good except some sort of knowledge.

Crito. Yes, you said that.

Socrates. Then the other results which a person might attribute to the statesman's art—and these, of course, would be numerous, as for instance, making the citizens rich and free and not disturbed by faction—all these appeared to be neither good nor evil;[62] but this art had to make them wise and to provide them with a share of knowledge if it was to be the one that

c   benefited them and made them happy.

Crito. True enough. So you agreed on this for the moment at any rate, according to your account.

Socrates. And does the kingly art make men wise and good?

Crito. Why not, Socrates?

Socrates. But does it make all people good, and in every respect? And is it the art which conveys every sort of knowledge, shoe making and carpentry and all the rest?

Crito. I don't think so, Socrates.

D   *Socrates.* Then what knowledge does it convey? And what use are we to make of it? It must not be the producer of any of those results which are neither good nor bad, but it must convey a knowledge which is none other than itself. Now shall we try to say what in the world this is, and what use we are to make of it? Is it agreeable to you if we say it is that by which we shall make others good?

Crito. Certainly.

Socrates. And in what respect will they be good and in what respect useful, as far as we are concerned? Or shall we go on to say that they will make others good and that these others will

E   do the same to still others? But in what conceivable way they are good is in no way apparent to us, especially since we have discredited what are said to be the results of the statesman's art.

62 Cf. 281DE.

It is altogether a case of the proverbial "Corinthus, son of Zeus";[63] and, as I was saying, we are in just as great difficulties as ever, or even worse, when it comes to finding out what that knowledge is which will make us happy.[64]

Crito. Mercy on us, Socrates, you seem to have got yourselves into a frightful tangle.

Socrates. As far as I was concerned, Crito, when I had fallen into this difficulty, I began to exclaim at the top of my lungs 293A and to call upon the two strangers as though they were the Heavenly Twins to rescue both myself and the boy from the great flood[65] of the argument and to endeavor in every conceivable way to make plain what this knowledge can be which we ought to have if we are going to spend the remainder of our lives in the right way.

Crito. And what about it? Was Euthydemus willing to reveal anything to you?

Socrates. Of course! And he began his account, my friend, in SCENE V this generous manner: Would you prefer, Socrates, to have me B teach you this knowledge you have been in difficulties over all this time, or to demonstrate that you possess it?

O marvellous man, I said, is this in your power?

Very much so, he said.

Then for heaven's sake demonstrate that I possess it! I said. That will be much easier than learning for a man of my age.

Then come answer me this, he said: Is there anything you know?

[63] The expression was proverbial for any sort of vain repetition. The scholiast's explanation is that when the Corinthian colony of Megara revolted from its mother city, the Corinthians sent ambassadors to appeal (repeatedly and unsuccessfully) to Megarian sentiment for the mythical founder of the colony, "Corinthus, son of Zeus." The scholiast on Pindar, *Nemean* VII. 104–105, gives both this story and one concerning Aletes.

[64] This passage (291C–292E) concerning the failure of the kingly art to meet the requirements laid down should be compared with the difficulties concerning temperance in the *Charmides* 173A ff. and the nature of the friend in the *Lysis* 219B ff.

[65] Literally the "third wave," which was traditionally the largest. (Cf. the well-known passage in *Republic* V. 472A.) The Dioscuri were regarded as protectors of seamen.

Oh, yes, I said, many things, though trivial ones.

That will serve the purpose, he said. Now do you suppose it possible for any existing thing not to be what it is?

293C Heavens no, not I.

And do you know something? he said.

Yes, I do.

Then you are knowing, if you really know?

Of course, as far as concerns that particular thing.

That doesn't matter, because mustn't you necessarily know everything, if you are knowing?

How in heaven's name can that be, said I, when there are many other things I don't know?

Then if there is anything you don't know, you are not knowing.

In just that matter, my friend, I said.

Are you any the less not knowing for all that? said he. And just now you said you were knowing, with the result that you are the man you are, and then again you are not, at the same
D time and in respect to the same things.⁶⁶

Very good, Euthydemus—according to the proverb, "whatever you say is well said."⁶⁷ But how do I know that knowledge we were looking for? Since it is impossible both to be and not to be the same thing, if I know one thing I know absolutely everything—because I could not be both knowing and not knowing at the same time—and since I know everything, I also have this knowledge. Is this what you mean, and is this your piece of wisdom?⁶⁸

66 This seems a clear reference to the principle of noncontradiction, and one not usually noted. Cf. *Republic* IV, 436B and, of course, Aristotle, *Metaphysics* 1005b19–23. τοῦτο ἀδύνατόν . . . τε καὶ μή just below at 293D4–5 is probably a gloss; see U. V. Wilamowitz-Moellendorf, *Platon*. II (Berlin, 1962), p. 371.

67 Reading πάντα λέγεις with BTW; although a good case could also be made for πάντ᾽ ἄγεις ("you bring good news") with the scholiast of T.

68 Socrates has given a concise summary of the sophists' argument. The fallacy consists in moving from "knowing some one thing" to "knowing" in general (which implies knowing all things). As the same trick can also be worked for "not knowing," and, by the principle of noncontradiction, it is

You are refuted out of your own mouth, Socrates, he said. 293E

But Euthydemus, I said, aren't you in the same condition? Because I would not be at all vexed at anything I might suffer in company with you and this dear man Dionysodorus. Tell me, don't you two know some existing things, and aren't there others you don't know?

Far from it, Socrates, said Dionysodorus.

What's that? I said. Do you know nothing at all?

On the contrary, he said.

Then you know everything, I said, since you know some- 294A thing?

Yes, everything, he said, and you also know everything if you really know even one thing.

O heavens, said I, how marvellous! And what a great blessing has come to light! But it can't be true that all the rest of mankind either know everything or nothing?

Well, he said, I don't suppose they know some things and not others and are thus knowing and not knowing at the same time.

But what follows? I asked.

Everyone, he said, knows everything, if he really knows something.

By the gods, Dionysodorus, I said—for I realize that you are B both now in earnest, although I have provoked you to it with some difficulty—do you two really know everything? Carpentry and shoe making, for instance?

Yes indeed, he said.

So you are both able to do leather stitching?

Heavens yes, and we can do cobbling, he said.

And do you also have the sort of information which tells the number of the stars and of the sands?

---

impossible to be both knowing and not knowing at the same time, Socrates has the unpleasant choice either of proclaiming himself all-ignorant or else of acquiescing in the spurious omniscience with which Euthydemus would like to present him. That Plato understands where the difficulty lies can be seen from the objection made by Socrates at 293c6: if there is something he does not know, he is not knowing only "in just that matter." Aristotle describes the fallacy, traditionally known as that of *a dicto secundum quid ad dictum simpliciter*, in *On Sophistical Refutations* 166b38 ff.

Of course, he said. Do you think we would fail to agree to that too?

Here Ctesippus interrupted: For goodness' sake, Dionyso-
294C dorus, give me some evidence of these things which will convince me that you are both telling the truth.

What shall I show you? he asked.

Do you know how many teeth Euthydemus has, and does he know how many you have?

Aren't you satisfied, he said, with being told that we know everything?

Not at all, he answered, but tell us just this one thing in addition and prove that you speak the truth. Because if you say how many each of you has, and you turn out to be right when we have made a count, then we shall trust you in everything else.

D Well, they weren't willing to do it, since they thought they were being laughed at,[69] but they claimed to know every single thing they were questioned about by Ctesippus. And there was practically nothing Ctesippus did not ask them about in the end, inquiring shamelessly whether they knew the most disgraceful things. The two of them faced his questions very manfully, claiming to know in each case, just like boars when they are driven up to the attack.[70] The result was that even I myself, Crito, was finally compelled, out of sheer disbelief, to ask
E whether Dionysodorus even knew how to dance, to which he replied that he certainly did.

I don't suppose, I said, that at your age you are so far advanced in wisdom as to somersault over swords or be turned about on a wheel?

There is nothing I cannot do, he said.

And do you know everything just at the present moment, I asked, or is your knowledge also a permanent thing?

69 Their unwillingness, of course, springs also from their desire to remain on a purely verbal plane. Socrates, on the other hand, wants not just words but action; see his remarks to Cleinias at the conclusion of Scene II (282D).

70 In this respect the sophists hold out better than Polus and Callicles in the *Gorgias*. (See below, p. 47, note 73.)

It is permanent as well, he said.

And when you were children and had just been born, did you know everything?

They both answered yes at the same moment.

Now the thing struck us as unbelievable; and Euthydemus 295A asked, Are you incredulous, Socrates?

Well, I would be, I said, except for the probability that you are both wise men.

But if you are willing to answer my questions, he said, I will prove that you agree to these remarkable things too.

But, said I, there is nothing I would like better than to be refuted on these points. Because if I am unaware of my own wisdom, but you are going to demonstrate that I know everything and know it forever, what greater godsend than this would I be likely to come across my whole life long?

Then answer, he said.

Ask away, I am ready.[71]   B

Well then, Socrates, he said, when you have knowledge, do you have it of something, or not?

I have it of something.

And do you know by means of that by which you have knowledge, or by means of something else?

By means of that by which I have knowledge. I suppose you mean the soul, or isn't this what you have in mind?

[71] The sophist has previously established that Socrates is omniscient (knowing); now he goes on to establish that he is permanently in this condition. His method is to attach the word "always" to "know" in a phrase in which its natural meaning is "whenever." He then detaches a sufficient number of qualifications to shift the meaning of "whenever" to "forever." Thus at 296B his question "do you always know by this means?" should really be (as Socrates attempts to point out) "do you always know, whenever you know, by means of that by which you know, i.e., the soul?" (I have attempted to bring out the shift in meaning by inserting a comma after the word "know" when the question occurs the second time: "you always know, by this means" at 296B3.) The whole passage 293B–296B is an excellent example of the indirect exposure of a fallacious argument by Plato (to be contrasted with the direct explanation of the equivocation on "learn" at 277E–278B). The expansions which Socrates would like to supply are just those which provide the solution of the fallacy.

Aren't you ashamed, Socrates, he said, to be asking a question of your own when you ought to be answering?

Very well, said I, but how am I to act? I will do just what you tell me. Now whenever I don't understand your question, do you want me to answer just the same, without inquiring further about it?

295C You surely grasp something of what I say, don't you? he said.

Yes, I do, said I.

Then answer in terms of what you understand.

Well then, I said, if you ask a question with one thing in mind and I understand it with another and then answer in terms of the latter, will you be satisfied if I answer nothing to the purpose?

I shall be satisfied, he said, although I don't suppose *you* will.

Then I'm certainly not going to answer, said I, until I understand the question.

You are evading a question you understand all along, he said, because you keep talking nonsense and are practically senile.

D I realized he was angry with me for making distinctions in his phrases, because he wanted to surround me with words and so hunt me down. Then I remembered that Connus, too, is vexed with me whenever I don't give in to him, and that as a result, he takes fewer pains with me because he thinks I am stupid. And since I had made up my mind to attend this man's classes too, I thought I had better give in for fear he might think me too uncouth to be his pupil. So I said, Well, Euthy-

E demus, if you think this is how to do things, we must do them your way, because you are far more of an expert at discoursing than I, who have merely a layman's knowledge of the art. So go back and ask your questions from the beginning.

And you answer again from the beginning, he said. Do you know what you know by means of something, or not?

I know it by means of the soul, I said.

296A There he is again, he said, adding on something to the question! I didn't ask you by what you know, but whether you know by means of something.

Yes, I did give too much of an answer again, I said, because I am so uneducated. Please forgive me and I shall answer simply that I know what I know by means of something.

And do you always know by this same means, said he, or is it rather the case that you know sometimes by this means and sometimes by another?

Always, whenever I know, I said, it is by this means.

Won't you stop adding things on again? he said.

But I'm afraid that this word "always" may trip us up.

It won't do it to us, he said, but to you, if anyone. Come   296b
along and answer: do you always know by this means?

Always, I said, since I have to withdraw the "whenever."

Then you always know, by this means. And since you are always knowing, the next question is, do you know some things by this means by which you know and others by some other means, or everything by this one?

Absolutely everything by this one, said I—those that I know, that is.

There it is again, he said—here comes the same qualification.

Well I take back the "those that I know," I said.

No, don't take back a single thing, he said—I'm not asking you any favors. Just answer me this: would you be capable of knowing "absolutely everything," if you did not know every-   c
thing?

It would be remarkable if I did, said I.

And he said, Then add on anything you like now, because you admit that you know absolutely everything.

It seems I do, I said, especially since my "those that I know" has no effect, and I know everything.

And you have also admitted that you always know (by means of that by which you know), whenever you know, or however else you like to put it, because you have admitted that you always know and know all things at the same time. It is obvious that you knew even when you were a child and when you were being born and when you were being conceived. And before   d
you yourself came into being and before the foundation of

heaven and earth, you knew absolutely everything, if it is true
that you always know. And, by heaven, he said, you always will
know, and will know everything, if I want it that way.[72]

I hope you will want it that way, most honorable Euthydemus,
said I, if you are genuinely telling the truth. But I don't quite
believe in your ability to bring it off unless your brother Dionysodorus here should lend a helping hand—perhaps the two
of you might be able to do it. Tell me, I went on: with respect
296E to other things I see no possibility of disputing with men of
such prodigious wisdom by saying that I do not know everything, since you have stated that I do; but what about things
of this sort, Euthydemus—how shall I say I know that good
men are unjust? Come tell me, do I know this, or not?

Oh yes, you know it, he said.

Know what? said I.

That the good are not unjust.

297A   Yes, I've always known that, I said. But this isn't my question—what I'm asking is, where did I learn that the good *are*
unjust?

Nowhere, said Dionysodorus.

Then this is something I do not know, I said.

You are ruining the argument, said Euthydemus to Dionysodorus, and this fellow here will turn out to be not knowing,
and then he will be knowing and not knowing at the same time.
And Dionysodorus blushed.

But you, I said, what do you say, Euthydemus? Your all-know-
B   ing brother doesn't appear to be making a mistake, does he?[73]

---

72 In the *Cratylus* 386D Euthydemus is represented as holding the belief
that "everything belongs equally to everyone at the same time and always."
This doctrine is not precisely stated in our dialogue, but the present passage
contains a closely related view. Cf. also 299D.

73 In the brief passage 296E–297B Socrates really has the sophists on the
run. First he appears to accept their demonstration of his own omniscience,
but uses it to produce a conclusion which is too shocking for them to swal-
low: if he knows all things, these things include distasteful propositions such
as "the good are unjust." When Dionysodorus denies that Socrates knows
this, he is, of course, hoist by his own petard, since the sophists have
argued earlier that not to know one thing is to be "not knowing." If they

Am I a brother of Euthydemus? said Dionysodorus, interrupting quickly.

And I said, Let that pass, my good friend, until Euthydemus instructs me as to how I know that good men are unjust, and don't begrudge me this piece of information.

You are running away, Socrates, said Dionysodorus, and refusing to answer.

And with good reason, said I, because I am weaker than either of you, so that I do not hesitate to run away from you both together. I am much more worthless than Heracles, who   297c
was unable to fight it out with both the Hydra,[74] a kind of lady-sophist who was so clever that if anyone cut off one of her heads of argument, she put forth many more in its place, and with another sort of sophist, a crab arrived on shore from the sea—rather recently, I think. And when Heracles was in distress because this creature was chattering and biting on his left, he called for his nephew Iolaus to come and help him, which Iolaus successfully did. But if my Iolaus[75] should come, he   D
would do more harm than good.

---

now stick to this, they are transgressing the principle of noncontradiction which they themselves invoked at 293CD, as Euthydemus promptly points out to his less nimble-minded brother at 297A. (This technique of pushing an argument to a shocking conclusion is one that Plato employs on various occasions. Cf. *Gorgias* 474C, where Polus is not ready to deny that doing wrong is fouler than suffering it and thus fails to escape Socrates' conclusion that it must be more evil as well [475D]. The supposedly shameless Callicles expatiates on this point at 482C ff., but he himself is shocked when Socrates wants to introduce catamites into a discussion of pleasure at 494C ff.) Then when Euthydemus reprimands his brother for spoiling the argument, Socrates is able to remind them of their position concerning mistakes (287A).

[74] The Hydra was a poisonous water snake with numerous heads; when one was cut off, others grew in its place. When Heracles was fighting with the Hydra, Hera sent a crab to its assistance, hence the proverb, alluded to at 297B10, that "not even Heracles fights against two." Heracles ultimately won the fight with the help of his nephew Iolaus. (Cf. *Phaedo* 89C.) From the seating order described at 271B we can identify the recently arrived crab with Dionysodorus, which makes Euthydemus the Hydra.

[75] By "my Iolaus," Socrates apparently means Ctesippus, but if so it seems an ungrateful remark in view of his ally's services on the side of right.

And when you have finished this song and story, said Dionysodorus, will you tell me whether Iolaus is any more Heracles' nephew than yours?[76]

Well, I suppose it will be best for me if I answer you, Dionysodorus, I said, because you will not stop asking questions—I am quite convinced of that—out of an envious desire to prevent Euthydemus from teaching me that piece of wisdom.

Then answer, he said.

297E Well, I said, my answer is that Iolaus was the nephew of Heracles, but as for being mine, I don't see that he is, in any way whatsoever. Because my brother, Patrocles, was not his father, although Heracles' brother, Iphicles, does have a name which is somewhat similar.

And Patrocles, he said, is your brother?

Yes indeed, said I—we have the same mother, though not the same father.

Then he both is and is not your brother.

Not by the same father, my good friend, I said, because his father was Chaeredemus and mine was Sophroniscus.

But Sophroniscus and Chaeredemus were both fathers? he asked.

298A Certainly, I said—the former was mine and the latter his.

Then was Chaeredemus other than a father? he said.

Other than mine at any rate, said I.

Then he was a father while he was other than a father? Or are you the same as a stone?[77]

I'm afraid you will show that I am, I said, although I don't feel like one.

Then are you other than a stone? he said.

Yes, quite other.

Then isn't it the case that if you are other than a stone, you are not a stone, he said, and if you are other than gold, you are not gold?

[76] The point of this question seems to be to lead Socrates to mention his half brother Patrocles and thus to pave the way for the next series of arguments involving Sophroniscus and Chaeredemus.

[77] To call someone a stone was to label him stupid and insensitive. Cf. *Gorgias* 494A.

That's true.

Then Chaeredemus is not a father if he is other than a father, he said.

So it seems that he is not a father, said I.

Because if Chaeredemus *is* a father, said Euthydemus, inter- 298B rupting, then, on the other hand, Sophroniscus, being other than a father, is not a father, so that you, Socrates, are without a father.[78]

Here Ctesippus took up the argument, saying, Well, isn't your father in just the same situation? Isn't he other than my father?

Far from it, said Euthydemus.

What! Is he the same? he asked.

The same, certainly.

I should not agree with that. But tell me, Euthydemus, is he c just my father, or the father of everyone else as well?

Of everyone else as well, he replied. Or do you think the same man is both a father and not a father?[79]

I was certainly of that opinion, said Ctesippus.

What, he said—do you think that a thing can be both gold and not gold? Or both a man and not a man?

But perhaps, Euthydemus, said Ctesippus, you are not uniting flax with flax, as the proverb has it.[80] Because you are making an alarming statement if you say your father is the father of all.

[78] The move from "other than a stone" to "not a stone" appears unexceptionable, since no human being is a stone in any case. But when the same move is executed for "father," we can see that this is really a fallacious step, since to be other than a particular father is by no means the same as to be not a father absolutely. The fallacy belongs to the general family of *secundum quid* (see above, p. 40, note 68, on 293D). This whole series of arguments involving "same," "other," and "not" should certainly be studied in connection with the analysis of negation in the *Sophist*.

[79] Again the sophists are invoking the principle of noncontradiction; see above, 293D.

[80] The proverb means to combine like things, as in Aristotle, *Physics* 207a19. Ctesippus' objection that Euthydemus is combining things which are not really similar is well founded: what makes a man a father is the existence of a son, whereas a thing can be a man or gold quite apart from any external relationship. Thus the principle of noncontradiction cannot be applied in the same way.

But he is, he replied.

Just of men, said Ctesippus, or of horses and all the other animals?

298D   All of them, he said.

And is your mother their mother?

Yes, she is.

And is your mother the mother of sea urchins?

Yes, and so is yours, he said.

So you are the brother of gudgeons and puppies and piglets.

Yes, and so are you, he said.

And your father turns out to be a boar and a dog.

And so does yours, he said.

You will admit all this in a moment, Ctesippus, if you answer my questions, said Dionysodorus. Tell me, have you got a dog?[81]

Yes, and a brute of a one too, said Ctesippus.

E   And has he got puppies?

Yes indeed, and they are just like him.

And so the dog is their father?

Yes, I saw him mounting the bitch myself, he said.

Well then: isn't the dog yours?

Certainly, he said.

Then since he is a father and is yours, the dog turns out to be your father, and you are the brother of puppies, aren't you?

And again Dionysodorus[82] cut in quickly to keep Ctesippus

81 The pattern of argument changes here. Euthydemus has just been developing the consequences of absolute fatherhood (which involves some interesting family connections); now Dionysodorus produces one of the same conclusions, that Ctesippus' father is a dog (cf. 298D5), by a different means, by the fallacy of composition. The argument runs more easily in Greek than in English: The dog is (a) father; the dog is your(s); the dog is your father. The fallacy could also be classified as one of those turning on accident. (See Aristotle, On Sophistical Refutations 179a35, where this particular argument is in fact mentioned.) But if a fallacy either of composition or of accident is to be brought off, there must be an accompanying equivocation; in other words, there would be no point in combining "your" with "father" unless an altered sense resulted from the collocation. Here the word "your" suggests, first, ownership and, secondly, blood relationship. For Plato's awareness of this point, see below on 299E.

82 It would make better sense both here and with what follows if Euthydemus were the speaker, but there is no textual evidence for the change.

from making some reply first and said, Just answer me one more small question: Do you beat this dog of yours?

And Ctesippus laughed and said, Heavens yes, since I can't beat you!

Then do you beat your own father? he asked.

There would certainly be much more reason for me to beat 299A yours, he said, for taking it into his head to beget such clever sons. But I suppose, Euthydemus, that the father of you and the puppies has benefited greatly from this wisdom of yours!

But he has no need of a lot of good things, Ctesippus—he does not, and neither do you.

Nor you either, Euthydemus? he asked.

Nor any other man. Tell me, Ctesippus, do you think it a good thing for a sick man to drink medicine whenever he needs B it, or does it seem to you not a good thing? And do you think it good for a man to be armed when he goes to war rather than to go unarmed?

It seems good to me, he said. And yet I think you are about to play one of your charming tricks.

The best way to find out is to go ahead and answer, he said. Since you admit that it is a good thing for a man to drink medicine whenever he needs it, then oughtn't he to drink as much as possible? And won't it be fine if someone pounds up and mixes him a wagon load of hellebore?[83]

And Ctesippus said, Very true indeed, Euthydemus, if the man drinking is as big as the statue at Delphi![84] C

It also follows, he said, that since it is a good thing to be armed in war, that a man ought to have as many spears and shields as possible, if it really is a good thing?

It really does seem to be so, said Ctesippus. But surely you

---

[83] This is *a dicto simpliciter ad dictum secundum quid*. (See above, p. 40, note 68, for the reverse.) Ctesippus' admission that the taking of medicine is in general good for a sick man is utilized in some particular ridiculous way. But see also Aristotle, *Rhetoric* 1401a32, on composition and division in a similar context.

[84] It does not seem possible to identify this statue precisely; perhaps it is the one erected by the Greeks after the battle of Salamis. See Pausanias, X. 14. 3, and Herodotus, VIII. 121.

don't believe this yourself, Euthydemus? Wouldn't you prefer one shield and one spear?[85]

Yes, I would.

And would you also arm Geryon and Briareus[86] in this fashion? he asked. I thought you and your companion here were cleverer than that, considering that you both fight in armor.

Euthydemus was silent, but Dionysodorus went back to the
299D answers Ctesippus had given earlier and asked, And what about gold, then? In your opinion is it a good thing to have?

Yes indeed, and, in this case, lots of it, said Ctesippus.

Well then, oughtn't one to have good things always and everywhere?

Very much so, he said.

And you admit that gold is also one of the good things?

Yes, I have admitted that already, he said.

Then one should have it always and everywhere, and especially in oneself? And wouldn't a man be happiest of all if he
E had three talents of gold in his stomach, and a talent in his skull, and a stater of gold in each eye?

Well, they do say, Euthydemus, said Ctesippus, that among the Scythians the happiest and best are the men who have a lot of gold in their own skulls (the same way that you were talking a moment ago about the dog being my father); and, what is still more remarkable, the story is that they also drink out of their own gilded skulls and gaze at the insides of them, having their own heads in their hands![87]

85 This passage has been called in evidence for the fact that one spear was the normal equipment of the hoplite by the late fifth century. (See Anthony Snodgrass, *Early Greek Armour and Weapons* [Edinburgh, 1964], p. 184.)

86 Briareus was one of the hundred-handed monsters, sons of Heaven and Earth, who aided Zeus against the Titans. Geryon was a three-headed or three-bodied monster whose cattle were stolen by Heracles. Cf. *Gorgias* 484BC.

87 The Scythians' habit of using the gilded skulls of their enemies as cups is described by Herodotus, IV. 65, and in the *Dissoi Logoi* II. 13. Ctesippus' point is that this is another case in which there is ambiguity in a possessive adjective. As "your" does not mean the same thing when applied to "dog" as it does when applied to "father," so "their" means something different

Tell me, said Euthydemus, do the Scythians and the rest of 300A
mankind see things capable of sight or incapable?[88]
Capable, I suppose.
And do you do so too? he asked.
Yes, so do I.
And do you see our cloaks?
Yes.
Then these same cloaks are capable of sight.
Remarkably so, said Ctesippus.[89]
Well, what do they see? he said.
Nothing at all. And you, perhaps, don't suppose you see
them,[90] you are such a sweet innocent. But you strike me, Euthy-
demus, as having fallen asleep with your eyes open; and if it
is possible to speak and say nothing, you are doing exactly
that.[91]
But surely it is not possible for there to be a speaking of the B
silent, said Dionysodorus.[92]

---

when applied to a skull which is owned (1) as a part of the owner's body
and (2) as an independent possession.

[88] It is practically impossible to reproduce the phrase *dunata horan* in
English so as to bring out the fact that it can be understood as either active
(capable of seeing) or passive (capable of being seen). The fallacy proceeds
by selecting an inanimate object, and then, after gaining the admission that
this object can be seen (passive), by shifting to the active sense and claiming
that the object can see. Ctesippus, however, refuses to admit the active sense.

[89] Apparently there was something unusual about the sophists' mode of
dress.

[90] Reading ὁρᾶν αὐτά with T.

[91] Literally, "if it is possible for the speaking to speak nothing." It seems
to be Ctesippus' use of this phrase involving an accusative participle with
an infinitive (*legonta legein*) which suggests the argument about the speaking of the silent which follows. (See below, note 92.)

[92] This next argument, which is in two parts, is based on the Greek construction in which, after certain verbs, an accusative is subject of an infinitive. (It was a similar construction that contributed to the success of the
Delphic oracle: in "the god says the Greeks the Persians will destroy," it is
impossible to tell which side is subject and which is object.) Here, with the
phrase *sigōnta legein*, the meaning could be either (1) it is impossible that
the silent (i.e., the dumb) should speak, or (2) it is impossible to speak concerning the silent. The sophist uses not only the *sigōnta legein* phrase but

Entirely impossible, said Ctesippus.

Then neither is there a silence of the speaking?

Still less so, he answered.

But whenever you mention stones and wood and pieces of iron, are you not speaking of the silent?[93]

Not if I go by the blacksmiths' shops, he said, because there the pieces of iron are said to speak out and cry aloud if anyone handles them. So here, thanks to your wisdom, you were talking nonsense without being aware of it. But prove me the other point, how there can be a silence of the speaking.

300c   (I had the notion that Ctesippus was very much keyed up on account of his favorite being there.)

Whenever you are silent, said Euthydemus, are you not silent with respect to all things?

Yes, I am, he said.

Therefore, you are also silent with respect to the speaking, if "the speaking" is included in all things.

What, said Ctesippus, all things are not silent, are they?[94]

---

also its converse, *legonta sigan*, at 300B3. (The verb which appeared as accusative participle becomes infinitive and vice versa.) The two senses are (1) it is impossible that the speaking should be silent, and (2) it is impossible to be silent concerning the speaking. In the case of both phrases the first sense is one to which a person would reasonably object; when the shift is made to the perfectly reasonable second sense, he can be made to look silly.

93 The sophist is interleaving his arguments; he is now working with *sigōnta legein* (mentioned first), not with *legonta sigan*. He has shifted the meaning to the second sense but Ctesippus retorts by suggesting a possible case for the first sense. (For the two senses see above, note 92.) Ctesippus then goes on to ask for the *legonta sigan* argument. (Note his assumption that since he has been made to admit that this was *not* possible, the sophist will be prepared to show that it *is*.)

94 Ctesippus' objection is not very clear, but I would suggest the following interpretation: Euthydemus' use of the word *panta* (all things), a neuter plural like *sigōnta* and *legonta* for which the accusative and nominative are the same, suggests to Ctesippus that he can easily construct an argument of his own with *panta* and the infinitive *sigan*. The two meanings would be (1) it is possible to be silent with respect to all things (Euthydemus has just said this at 300c2), and (2) it is possible for all things to be silent (this is Ctesippus' contribution at c4–5). As a result of his essay into sophistry he has the satisfaction of placing Euthydemus in a position in which he must

I imagine not, said Euthydemus.

Well then, my good friend, do all things speak?

All the speaking ones, I suppose.

But, he said, this is not my question—I want to know, are all things silent, or do they speak?

Neither and both, said Dionysodorus, breaking in, and I'm convinced you will be helpless in dealing with that answer. 300D

Ctesippus gave one of his tremendous laughs and said, Euthydemus, your brother has made the argument sit on both sides of the fence and it is ruined and done for! Cleinias was very pleased and laughed too, which made Ctesippus swell to ten times his normal size. It is my opinion that Ctesippus, who is a bit of a rogue, had picked up these very things by overhearing these very men, because there is no wisdom of a comparable sort among any other persons of the present day.

And I said, Cleinias, why are you laughing at such serious and E beautiful things?

Why Socrates, have you ever yet seen a beautiful thing? asked Dionysodorus.[95]

---

either answer "yes" to the question, "Do all things speak?" (as a result of having answered "no" to the previous one as to whether all things are silent), or he must (as Gifford points out) "limit the universal term τὰ πάντα by a distinction such as he would not allow Socrates to use 295B4, 296A1." (E. H. Gifford, *The Euthydemus of Plato* [Oxford, 1905], *ad loc*.) Euthydemus does the latter at c6. Dionysodorus with his "neither and both" is answering Ctesippus' question with yes *and* no, thus breaking a rule tacitly assumed by the sophists themselves, that every question must be answered yes *or* no.

[95] Since the important article of G. Vlastos ("The Third Man Argument in the *Parmenides*," *Philosophical Review*, LXIII [1954], 319–349), the self-predication discussion has centred on the *Parmenides* with a few side glances at the *Protagoras* and *Phaedo*. But *Euthydemus* 300E–301C should have its place in the discussion too, as an analysis of the passage will quickly show. At 300E ff. Dionysodorus has made an attack on the theory of Forms which is apparently Eleatic in origin. He asks Socrates (1) whether he has ever seen a beautiful thing, and (2) whether these beautiful things were different from the beautiful or the same as the beautiful. We can guess, from the type of fallacious argument put forward by Dionysodorus and his brother earlier in the dialogue, what the plan of attack is most likely to be. Socrates is required to choose one of the proffered alternatives, either that the (particular)

Yes indeed, Dionysodorus, I said, and many of them.

301A   And were they different from the beautiful, he asked, or were
they the same as the beautiful?

This put me in a terrible fix, which I thought I deserved for

---

beautiful things are the same as (identical with) the beautiful, or that they
are (totally) different from it. Whichever alternative he chooses, he will play
into the sophist's hands: if he says they are the same as the beautiful,
Dionysodorus can conclude that there are no beautiful things since there is
no distinction between them and the beautiful; if he says they are different,
the sophist can draw the same conclusion by using (1) the other-not argument (298AC) and (2) the nonexistence argument (283CD). (That is, he can
say that if the beautiful things are different from the beautiful then they are
not [the beautiful] and thus do not exist.) Socrates, however, chooses neither
horn of the dilemma; instead he attempts an escape between the horns by
replying, to Dionysodorus' question, that the beautiful things "were different
from the beautiful itself, but at the same time there was some beauty present with each of them." The sophist's response (and here we come to the
crucial passage) is first to make the ox joke at 301A, and then to answer,
cryptically indeed, "but in what way can the different be different just because the different is present with the different?" What he has done is to
substitute the one expression, "the different," for *both* the beautiful things
(which are different from the beautiful) *and* the beautiful (which is different
from the beautiful things). Thus his question in its full form should probably read "but in what way can the beautiful things be different (from the
beautiful) just because the beautiful is present with the beautiful things?"
As a matter of fact, this is a perfectly good and, indeed, important question
in connection with the idea of "presence." The sophist, however, has preferred to phrase his question in this misleading and elliptical way because,
as an Eleatic, he wishes to destroy the dualism implied in Socrates' answer.
Socrates has spoken of both "the beautiful" and "beautiful things"; by
referring to both under the same title, Dionysodorus has gotten rid of the
distinction between them. But he has, in the course of this maneuver, laid
himself open to an unexpected rejoinder from Socrates, who now proceeds
on the assumption that the expression "the different" is intended by Dionysodorus to be on a par with the beautiful, in other words, that it is a
Form. The sophist has asked, "in what way can the different be different?";
Socrates answers, "well, why not, if the beautiful is beautiful and the ugly
ugly?" In other words, he meets Dionysodorus' objection to the theory of
Forms by making it appear, by analogy, that Dionysodorus has himself been
using the language of Forms. Taken as a whole, the passage seems to me to
imply that "the different" cannot be a Form, or, at least, that it is not
to be included in the same class with Forms like "the beautiful." The re-
percussions for the *megista genē* of the *Sophist* are obvious.

my grumbling. All the same I answered that they were different from the beautiful itself, but at the same time there was some beauty present with each of them.

Then if an ox is present with you, you are an ox? And because I am present with you now, you are Dionysodorus?[96]

Heaven forbid, said I.

But in what way, he said, can the different be different just because the different is present with the different?

Are you in difficulties there? I said. (I was so eager to have 301B the wisdom of the pair that I was already trying to copy it.)

How can I not be in difficulties? he said. Not only I but everyone else must be, when a thing is impossible.

What are you saying, Dionysodorus? I said. Isn't the beautiful beautiful and the ugly ugly?

Yes, if I like, he said.

And do you like?

Certainly, he said.

Then isn't it also the case that the same is the same and the different different? Because I don't imagine that the different is the same, but I thought even a child would hardly doubt that c the different is different. But you must have neglected this point deliberately, Dionysodorus, since in every other respect you and your brother strike me as bringing the art of argument to a fine pitch of excellence, like craftsmen who bring to completion whatever work constitutes their proper business.

You know then, he said, what the proper business of each craftsman is?[97] For instance, you know whose business it is to work metal?

[96] This passage is relevant to the discussion of *parousia* in the *Lysis* 217B ff. and to the objections to the theory of Forms raised in the first part of the *Parmenides*. And perhaps Plato has objections of the ox type in mind when he has Socrates say in the *Phaedo* 100CE that the safest answer he can give to the question of "what makes a thing beautiful" is that "it is by beauty that beautiful things are beautiful."

[97] We now have another fallacious argument made possible by the Greek accusative and infinitive construction: *prosēkei mageiron sphattein* can mean either (1) it is proper for the cook to slaughter, or (2) it is proper to slaughter the cook, for instance.

Yes, I do—the blacksmith's.

Well then, what about making pots?

The potter's.

And again, to slaughter and skin, and to boil and roast the pieces after cutting them up?

301D The cook's, I said.

Now if a man does the proper business, he said, he will do rightly?

Very much so.

And the proper business in the case of the cook is, as you say, to cut up and skin? You did agree to that didn't you?

Yes, I did, I said, but forgive me.

Then it is clear, he said, that if someone kills the cook and cuts him up, and then boils him and roasts him, he will be doing the proper business. And if anyone hammers the blacksmith himself, and puts the potter on the wheel, he will also

E be doing the proper business.

By Poseidon, I exclaimed, you are putting the finishing touches on your wisdom! And do you think that such skill will ever be mine?

And would you recognize it, Socrates, he asked, if it did become yours?

If only you are willing, I said, I clearly would.

What's that, said he—do you think you know your own possessions?

Yes, unless you forbid it—for all my hopes must begin with you and end with Euthydemus here.[98]

And do you consider those things to be yours over which you have control and which you are allowed to treat as you please? For instance, an ox or a sheep: do you regard these as yours

302A because you are free to sell them or give them away or sacrifice them to any god you please? And if you could not treat them in this fashion, then they would not be yours?[99]

---

98 Socrates is imitating a common way of addressing a deity.

99 If this statement is meant to be deduced from the previous statement, a false conversion has occurred. But it could also be an independent statement intended to indicate an equivalence.

And because I knew that some fine thing would emerge from their questions, and, at the same time, because I wanted to hear it as quickly as possible, I said, This is exactly the case—it is only things like these which are mine.

Very well, he said. You give the name of living beings to all things that have a soul, don't you?

Yes, I said.

And you admit that only those living beings are yours over 302B which you have power to do all these things I mentioned just now?

I admit it.

And he pretended to pause as though he were contemplating some weighty matter, and then said, Tell me, Socrates, do you have an ancestral Zeus?[100]

I had a suspicion (a correct one as it turned out) of the way in which the argument would end, and I began to make a desperate effort to escape, twisting about as though I were already caught in the net.

No, I have not, Dionysodorus, I said.

Then you are a miserable sort of fellow, and not even an Athenian, if you have no ancestral gods nor shrines, nor any c of the other things of this sort which befit a gentleman.

Enough of that, Dionysodorus—mind your tongue and don't give me a lecture which is prematurely harsh. I certainly do have altars; and I have shrines, both domestic and ancestral, and everything else of the kind, just like the other Athenians.

Well, what about the other Athenians? he said. Doesn't each of them have an ancestral Zeus?

None of the Ionians use that expression, I said, neither those who are colonists from the city nor we ourselves. We do have an ancestral Apollo because of Ion's parentage,[101] but Zeus is not given the name of "ancestral" by us. Rather we call him "de- D

[100] Méridier points out (Budé edition, ad loc.) that patrōos as applied to Zeus has two senses: (1) father of the race; (2) protector of ancestors. Socrates tries to escape the ultimate conclusion of 303A by pretending to understand the epithet in the first rather than the second sense.

[101] Ion was the son of Apollo by Creusa. (Cf. Euripides, Ion, 61–75.)

fender of the house" or "of the tribe," and we also have an Athena "of the tribe."

Oh, that will do, said Dionysodorus, since you do appear to have an Apollo and a Zeus and an Athena.

Certainly, said I.

Then these would be your gods? he said.

My ancestors, I said, and my masters.

But at any rate they are yours, he said. Or didn't you admit that they were?

Yes, I admitted it, I said. What is going to happen to me?

Then these gods, he said, are also living beings? Because you
302E have admitted that everything which has a soul is a living being. Or don't these gods have a soul?[102]

Oh yes, they do, I said.

Then they are living beings?

Yes, living beings, I said.

And you have agreed that those living beings are yours which you have a right to give away and to sell and to sacrifice to any god you please.

Yes, I agreed to that, I said—there is no retreat for me, Euthydemus.

Then come tell me straightway, he said: since you admit that
303A Zeus and the other gods are yours, then do you have the right to sell them or give them away or treat them in any way you like, as you do with the other living creatures?[103]

Then I, Crito, lay speechless, just as if the argument had

[102] The argument is a first-figure syllogism in Barbara.

[103] The whole of this argument from 301E really turns on the ambiguity in "yours" and the other possessive adjectives. (We have already had a foretaste of this in the "your dog/your father" argument at 298D ff.) The possession of living creatures implies ownership and control; the possession of gods carries no such implication. (The classification of gods as living creatures involves some distortion of the word zōon, but this is subsidiary to the main equivocation.) Had Euthydemus and Dionysodorus been present at a performance of *The Pirates of Penzance*, they would have enjoyed the following passage in Act II: "*Major-General:* Frederic, in this chapel are ancestors: you cannot deny that. With the estate I bought the chapel and its contents. I don't know whose ancestors they *were*, but I know whose ancestors they *are.* . . ."

struck me a blow. But Ctesippus ran to my aid, saying, Bravo, Heracles, what a fine argument! And Dionysodorus said, Is Heracles a bravo, or is a bravo Heracles?[104] And Ctesippus said, By Poseidon, what marvellous arguments! I give up—the pair are unbeatable.

Whereupon, my dear Crito, there was no one there who did not praise to the skies the argument and the two men, laughing and applauding and exulting until they were nearly exhausted. In the case of each and every one of the previous arguments, it was only the admirers of Euthydemus who made such an enthusiastic uproar; but now it almost seemed as if the pillars of the Lyceum applauded the pair and took pleasure in their success. Even I myself was so affected by it as to declare that I had never in my life seen such wise men; and I was so absolutely captivated by their wisdom that I began to praise and extol them and said, O happy pair, what miraculous endowment you possess to have brought such a thing to perfection in so short a time! Among the many other fine things which belong to your arguments, Euthydemus and Dionysodorus, there is one which is the most magnificent of all, that you care nothing for the many, or in fact, for men of consequence or reputation, but only for persons of your own sort. And I am convinced that there are very few men like you who would appreciate these arguments, but that the majority understand them so little that I feel sure they would be more ashamed to refute others with arguments of this sort than to be refuted by them. And then there is this other public-spirited and kindly aspect of your performance; whenever you deny that there is anything beautiful or good or white, and that the different is in any way different,[105] you do in fact completely stitch up men's mouths, as you say. But since you would appear to stitch up your own as

303B

C

D

E

104 This final equivocation, which involves the shift of an adverb into a noun, and of an exclamation into a proper name, is the only totally ridiculous item in the dialogue. That Plato represents it as the climax of the sophists' display and as the maneuver which called forth the greatest applause can leave us in no doubt of his opinion of the eristic art.

105 This phrase is tentatively interpreted as a reference to the discussion at 301AC and is translated accordingly.

well, you are behaving in a charming fashion and the harshness of your words is quite removed.[106] But the greatest thing of all is that your skill is such, and is so skillfully contrived, that anyone can master it in a very short time. I myself found this out by watching Ctesippus and seeing how quickly he was able to imitate you on the spur of the moment. This ability of your technique to be picked up rapidly is a fine thing,[107] but not something which lends itself well to public performance. If you will take my advice, be careful not to talk in front of a large group; the listeners are likely to master it right away and give you no credit. Better just talk to each other in private, or, if you must have an audience, then let no one come unless he gives you money. And if you are sensible you will give your disciples the same advice, never to argue with anyone but yourselves and each other. For it is the rare thing, Euthydemus, which is the precious one, and water is cheapest, even though, as Pindar said, it is the best.[108] But come, said I, and see to admitting Cleinias and me to your classes.

After saying these things, Crito, and making a few other brief remarks, we separated. Now figure out a way to join us in attending their classes, since they claim to be able to instruct anyone who is willing to pay, and say that neither age nor lack of ability prevents anyone whatsoever from learning their wisdom easily. And, what is specially relevant for you to hear, they

---

[106] This is a very difficult passage, since it seems to say that Euthydemus and Dionysodorus have denied the existence of "anything beautiful or good or white" in the course of the display that Socrates has just recounted, and yet it is not easy to point to a precise passage in which they have done this. One possibility is that Socrates refers to 300E (Dionysodorus' question, "Why Socrates, have you ever yet seen a beautiful thing?") and that we are to assume that what would be true of beautiful things, which, on an Eleatic view, could not exist if the beautiful itself does so, would be likewise true for good things, white things, i.e., for all particulars. But this possibility does not make much sense in connection with Socrates' observation that the doctrine has the effect of stitching up not only the mouths of others but of its proponents as well; the only view which has been described as self-refuting is the one that there is no contradiction. (See 286c and 288A.)

[107] Omitting τὸ σοφόν with B.

[108] Olympian I.1.

say that their art is in no way a hindrance to the making of money.

Crito. Well, Socrates, I am indeed a person who loves listening and who would be glad to learn something; but all the same I am afraid that I also am not one of Euthydemus' sort. Instead I am one of those you mentioned who would rather be refuted 304D by arguments of this kind than use them to refute. Now it seems ridiculous to me to give you advice, but I want to tell you what I heard. When I was taking a walk one of the men who was leaving your discussion came up to me (someone who has a high opinion of himself for wisdom and is one of those clever people who write speeches for the law courts)[109] and he said, Crito, aren't you a disciple of these wise men? Heavens no, I said—there was such a crowd that I was unable to hear, even though I stood quite close. And yet, he said, it was worth hearing. What was it? I asked. You would have heard men con- E versing who are the wisest of the present day in this kind of argument. And I said, what did they show you? Nothing else, said he, than the sort of thing one can hear from such people at any time—chattering and making a worthless fuss about matters of no consequence. (These are his approximate words.) But surely, I said, philosophy is a charming thing. Charming, my innocent friend? he said—why it is of no value whatsoever! And 305A if you had been present, I think you would have been embarrassed on your friend's account, he acted so strangely in his willingness to put himself at the disposal of men who care nothing about what they say, but just snatch at every word. And these men, as I was just saying, are among the most influential people of the present day. But the fact is, Crito, he said, that both the activity itself and the men who engage in it are worthless and ridiculous. Now as far as I am concerned, Socrates, the man is wrong to criticize the activity and so is anyone else who does so. B But to be willing to argue with such people in front of a large crowd does seem to me worthy of reproach.

109 This is likely to be a reference to the orator Isocrates. But see also R. S. Bluck, *Plato's 'Meno'* (Cambridge, 1961), p. 115, note 4: ". . . probably this anonymous person is simply meant to represent a type."

Socrates. Crito, men like these are very strange. Still, I don't yet know what to say in return. What sort of man was this who came up and attacked philosophy? Was he one of those clever persons who contend in the law courts, an orator? Or was he one of those who equip such men for battle, a writer of the speeches which the orators use?

305c　*Crito.* He was certainly not an orator, no indeed. Nor do I think he has ever appeared in court. But they say he understands the business—very much so—and that he is a clever man and can compose clever speeches.[110]

Socrates. Now I understand—it was about this sort of person that I was just going to speak myself. These are the persons, Crito, whom Prodicus describes as occupying the no-man's-land between the philosopher and the statesman. They think that they are the wisest of men, and that they not only are but also seem to be so in the eyes of a great many, so that no one else

D　keeps them from enjoying universal esteem except the followers of philosophy. Therefore, they think that if they place these persons in the position of appearing to be worth nothing, then victory in the contest for the reputation of wisdom will be indisputably and immediately theirs, and in the eyes of all. They think they really are the wisest, and whenever they are cut short in private conversation, they attribute this to Euthydemus and his crew. They regard themselves as very wise, and reasonably so, since they think they are not only pretty well up in philosophy but also in politics. Yes, their conceit of wisdom is quite

E　natural because they think they have as much of each as they need; and, keeping clear of both risk and conflict, they reap the fruits of wisdom.

Crito. And so, Socrates, do you think there is anything in what they say? For surely it can't be denied that their argument has a certain plausibility.

Socrates. Plausibility is just what it does have, Crito, rather

306a　than truth. It is no easy matter to persuade them that a man or anything else which is between two things and partakes of

---

110 The person in question is clearly not one of those who know how to use what they have made; cf. 289D ff.

both is worse than one and better than the other in the case where one of the things is good and the other evil; and that in the case where it partakes of two distinct goods, it is worse than either of them with respect to the end for which each of the two (of which it is composed) is useful. It is only in the case where the thing in the middle partakes of two distinct evils that it is better than either of those of which it has a share.[111] Now   306B if philosophy is a good, and so is the activity of a statesman (and each has a different end), and those partaking of both are in between, then these men are talking nonsense, since they are inferior to both. If one is good and the other bad, then they are better than the practitioners of the latter and worse than those of the former; while if both are bad, there is some truth in what they say, but otherwise none at all. I don't suppose they would agree that both [philosophy and politics] are bad,   c nor that one is bad and the other good. The fact of the matter is that, while partaking of both, they are inferior to both with respect to the object for which either politics or philosophy is of value; and that whereas they are actually in the third place, they want to be regarded as being in the first. However, we ought to forgive them their ambition and not feel angry, although we still ought to see these men for what they are. After all, we ought to admire every man who says anything sensible, and who labors bravely in its pursuit.   D

Crito. All the same, Socrates, as I keep telling you, I am in doubt about what I ought to do with my sons. The younger one is still quite small, but Critobulus is at an age when he needs someone who will do him good. Now whenever I am in your company your presence has the effect of leading me to think it madness to have taken such pains about my children in various other ways, such as marrying to make sure that they   E would be of noble birth on the mother's side, and making money so that they would be as well off as possible, and then to give no thought to their education. But on the other hand, whenever I take a look at any of those persons who set up to

111 Possibly there is some anticipation of Aristotle's doctrine of the mean in this passage.

educate men, I am amazed; and every last one of them strikes
307A me as utterly grotesque, to speak frankly between ourselves. So
the result is that I cannot see how I am to persuade the boy to
take up philosophy.

Socrates. My dear Crito, don't you realize that in every pursuit most of the practitioners are paltry and of no account
whereas the serious men are few and beyond price? For instance,
doesn't gymnastics strike you as a fine thing? And money making and rhetoric and the art of the general?

Crito. Yes, of course they do.

Socrates. Well then: in each of these cases don't you notice
B that the majority give a laughable performance of their respec-
tive tasks?

Crito. Yes indeed—you are speaking the exact truth.

Socrates. And just because this is so, do you intend to run
away from all these pursuits and entrust your son to none of
them?

Crito. No, this would not be reasonable, Socrates.

Socrates. Then don't do what you ought not to, Crito, but
pay no attention to the practitioners of philosophy, whether
good or bad. Rather give serious consideration to the thing it-
C self: if it seems to you negligible, then turn everyone from it,
not just your sons. But if it seems to you to be what I think it is,
then take heart, pursue it, practice it, both you and yours, as
the proverb says.

Index